U.S. INTERNATIONAL TRADE IN GOODS AND SERVICES

The U.S. Census Bureau and the U.S. Bureau of Economic Analysis, through the Department of Commerce, announced today that the goods and services deficit was **$39.0 billion** in November, down $3.2 billion from $42.2 billion in October, revised. November exports were **$196.4 billion**, $2.0 billion less than October exports. November imports were **$235.4 billion**, $5.2 billion less than October imports.

The November decrease in the goods and services deficit reflected a decrease in the goods deficit of $3.3 billion to $58.3 billion and a decrease in the services surplus of $0.1 billion to $19.3 billion.

Year-to-date, the goods and services deficit increased $22.3 billion, or 5.1 percent, from the same period in 2013. Exports increased $60.0 billion or 2.9 percent. Imports increased $82.4 billion or 3.3 percent.

Goods and Services Three-Month Moving Averages (Exhibit 2)

The average goods and services deficit decreased $0.3 billion to $41.6 billion for the three months ending in November.

- Average exports of goods and services decreased $0.8 billion to $196.6 billion in November.
- Average imports of goods and services decreased $1.1 billion to $238.3 billion in November.

Year-over-year, the average goods and services deficit increased $2.5 billion from the three months ending in November 2013.

- Average exports of goods and services increased $3.6 billion from November 2013.
- Average imports of goods and services increased $6.1 billion from November 2013.

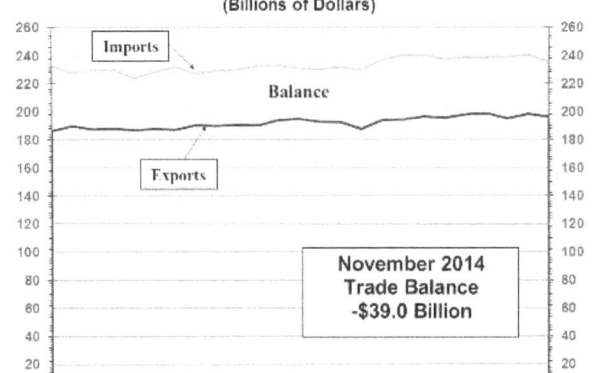

U.S. International Trade in Goods and Services
(Billions of Dollars)

November 2014
Trade Balance
-$39.0 Billion

Goods and Services Trade Balance
(Billions of Dollars)

November 2014

Monthly Balance	Three-Month Moving Average
-$39.0 Billion	-$41.6 Billion

NOTE: All statistics referenced are seasonally adjusted; statistics are on a balance of payments basis unless otherwise specified. Additional statistics, including not seasonally adjusted statistics and details for goods on a Census basis, are available in Exhibits 1-20b of this release. For information on data sources, definitions, and scheduled release dates through December 2015, see the information section on page A-1 of this release. The next release is **February 5, 2015.**

Exports (Exhibits 3, 6, and 7)

Exports of goods decreased $1.8 billion to $136.7 billion in November.
> *Exports of goods on a Census basis* decreased $1.9 billion.
> * Capital goods decreased $2.3 billion.
>   * o Civilian aircraft decreased $1.1 billion.
>   * o Generators, transformers, and accessories decreased $0.3 billion.
> *Net balance of payments adjustments* increased $0.1 billion.

Exports of services decreased $0.1 billion to $59.6 billion in November. The decrease mostly reflected a decrease in transport ($0.1 billion), which includes freight and port services and passenger fares.

Imports (Exhibits 4, 6, and 8)

Imports of goods decreased $5.2 billion to $195.0 billion in November.
> *Imports of goods on a Census basis* decreased $5.2 billion.
> * Industrial supplies and materials decreased $4.6 billion.
>   * o Crude oil decreased $2.2 billion.
>   * o Fuel oil decreased $0.7 billion.
> *Net balance of payments adjustments* decreased less than $0.1 billion.

Imports of services decreased less than $0.1 billion to $40.4 billion in November. A decrease in travel (for all purposes including education) ($0.1 billion) was mostly offset by increases of less than $0.1 billion in several categories of services.

Real Goods in 2009 Dollars – Census Basis (Exhibit 11)

The real goods deficit decreased $2.2 billion to $47.8 billion in November.

* Real exports of goods decreased $0.6 billion to $123.5 billion.
* Real imports of goods decreased $2.8 billion to $171.4 billion.

Revisions

Revisions to October exports
* Exports of goods were revised upward $0.5 billion.
* Exports of services were revised upward $0.2 billion.

Revisions to October imports
* Imports of goods were revised downward $0.5 billion.
* Imports of services were revised upward $0.1 billion.

Goods by Selected Countries and Areas: Monthly – Census Basis (Exhibit 19)

The November figures show surpluses, in billions of dollars, with South and Central America ($4.3) and Brazil ($0.6). Deficits were recorded, in billions of dollars, with China ($29.8), European Union ($12.7), Germany ($6.3), Japan ($5.6), Mexico ($4.4), South Korea ($2.9), Italy ($2.3), India ($1.7), France ($1.6), OPEC ($1.6), Canada ($1.4), Saudi Arabia ($1.3), and United Kingdom ($0.2).

* The deficit with **China** increased $0.2 billion to $29.8 billion in November. Exports decreased $0.2 billion to $11.1 billion and imports decreased $0.1 billion to $40.9 billion.

* The deficit with the **European Union** increased $1.5 billion to $12.7 billion in November. Exports decreased $0.7 billion to $22.2 billion and imports increased $0.8 billion to $35.0 billion.

NOTICE

Upcoming Changes to the FT-900 and the FT-900 Supplement

With the release of the "U.S. International Trade in Goods and Services: January 2015" report (FT-900) and the accompanying FT-900 Supplement on March 6, 2015, the following changes will be made:

- Exhibit 3 of the FT-900 Supplement, "General Imports of Crude Oil by Country," will be moved to the FT-900 and will be numbered Exhibit 17a. The content of this exhibit will not change.
- Exhibit 4 of the FT-900 Supplement, "Exports and Imports of Goods by SITC Commodity Sections," will be eliminated because the data in this exhibit are available in Exhibit 15 of the FT-900.
- Exhibits 5, 6, and 6a of the FT-900 Supplement will be renumbered Exhibits 3, 4, and 4a, respectively.
- The Euro Area will include Lithuania, which joined on January 1, 2015. This change will affect Exhibit 14 of the FT-900 and Exhibit 4 (current Exhibit 6) of the FT-900 Supplement.

If you have questions or need additional information, please contact the International Trade Indicator Macro Analysis Branch of the U.S. Census Bureau's Economic Indicators Division on (301) 763-2311 or at ftd.data.dissemination@census.gov.

BLANK PAGE

Table of Contents

Part A: Seasonally Adjusted (by Commodity/Service)

Exhibit 1. U.S. International Trade in Goods and Services

In millions of dollars. Details may not equal totals due to seasonal adjustment and rounding. (R) - Revised.

Period	Balance			Exports			Imports		
	Total	Goods (1)	Services	Total	Goods (1)	Services	Total	Goods (1)	Services
2012									
Jan. - Dec.	-537,605	-742,095	204,490	2,216,540	1,561,689	654,850	2,754,145	2,303,785	450,360
Jan. - Nov.	-499,972	-685,671	185,699	2,026,775	1,428,757	598,018	2,526,747	2,114,428	412,319
January	-51,266	-66,927	15,661	179,606	127,140	52,466	230,873	194,068	36,805
February	-43,338	-59,838	16,499	181,720	128,281	53,439	225,058	188,119	36,940
March	-49,850	-66,673	16,824	186,257	132,195	54,063	236,107	198,868	37,239
April	-47,773	-64,375	16,601	184,543	130,545	53,998	232,317	194,920	37,397
May	-47,184	-63,928	16,744	184,306	130,100	54,206	231,490	194,028	37,462
June	-43,078	-59,936	16,858	185,330	131,119	54,211	228,408	191,055	37,353
July	-43,834	-59,939	16,105	183,673	130,026	53,647	227,507	189,965	37,542
August	-44,536	-61,411	16,875	182,845	128,309	54,536	227,380	189,720	37,661
September	-40,150	-57,593	17,442	188,696	133,663	55,033	228,846	191,256	37,591
October	-42,358	-60,163	17,805	183,512	127,682	55,830	225,870	187,845	38,025
November	-46,604	-64,888	18,283	186,286	129,697	56,589	232,891	194,585	38,306
December	-37,634	-56,424	18,791	189,765	132,932	56,833	227,399	189,357	38,042
2013									
Jan. - Dec.	-476,392	-701,669	225,276	2,280,194	1,592,784	687,410	2,756,586	2,294,453	462,134
Jan. - Nov.	-438,999	-645,086	206,087	2,087,395	1,458,574	628,821	2,526,394	2,103,660	422,734
January	-42,205	-61,192	18,987	187,478	130,653	56,825	229,683	191,846	37,838
February	-41,770	-60,688	18,917	188,030	131,420	56,610	229,800	192,107	37,693
March	-36,973	-55,680	18,707	186,903	130,532	56,371	223,876	186,211	37,665
April	-40,417	-58,758	18,342	187,763	131,326	56,437	228,180	190,084	38,096
May	-44,831	-63,352	18,521	187,206	130,319	56,887	232,037	193,671	38,366
June	-36,552	-54,973	18,421	190,366	133,343	57,023	226,918	188,316	38,602
July	-39,419	-58,021	18,603	189,902	132,830	57,072	229,321	190,851	38,470
August	-39,515	-58,527	19,012	190,606	132,829	57,777	230,121	191,356	38,765
September	-42,263	-61,387	19,125	190,249	132,430	57,819	232,512	193,817	38,695
October	-39,083	-57,742	18,659	193,971	136,141	57,829	233,053	193,884	39,170
November	-35,972	-54,765	18,793	194,922	136,752	58,170	230,894	191,517	39,377
December	-37,393	-56,583	19,189	192,799	134,210	58,590	230,193	190,792	39,400
2014									
Jan. - Nov.	-461,336	-673,612	212,277	2,147,441	1,497,694	649,747	2,608,777	2,171,307	437,470
January	-39,181	-59,469	20,288	192,475	133,561	58,914	231,655	193,029	38,626
February	-42,230	-60,311	18,081	187,773	130,367	57,405	230,003	190,679	39,324
March	-43,124	-62,558	19,434	193,940	135,608	58,332	237,064	198,166	38,898
April	-45,914	-65,599	19,685	194,318	135,096	59,222	240,233	200,695	39,538
May	-43,562	-63,107	19,545	196,559	136,933	59,626	240,121	200,040	40,081
June	-41,745	-60,605	18,860	195,698	136,685	59,013	237,443	197,290	40,153
July	-40,695	-59,576	18,881	198,031	139,069	58,962	238,726	198,645	40,081
August	-40,031	-59,795	19,764	198,736	139,027	59,709	238,767	198,822	39,945
September	-43,603	-62,700	19,097	195,232	136,038	59,194	238,835	198,739	40,096
October (R)	-42,249	-61,613	19,364	198,321	138,580	59,742	240,570	200,192	40,378
November	-39,001	-58,279	19,277	196,357	136,730	59,627	235,359	195,009	40,350
December									

October data as published last month:

	-43,432	-62,671	19,239	197,537	138,045	59,493	240,970	200,716	40,253

(1) Data are presented on a balance of payments (BOP) basis.

NOTE: For information on data sources and methodology, see the information section on page A-1 of this release or at www.census.gov/ft900 or www.bea.gov/newsreleases/international/trade/tradnewsrelease.htm.

Part A: Seasonally Adjusted (by Commodity/Service)

Exhibit 2. U.S. International Trade in Goods and Services
Three-Month Moving Averages

In millions of dollars. Details may not equal totals due to seasonal adjustment and rounding. (R) - Revised.

Month of Moving Average	Balance			Exports			Imports		
	Total	Goods (1)	Services	Total	Goods (1)	Services	Total	Goods (1)	Services
2012									
January	-49,257	-65,036	15,779	179,903	127,359	52,543	229,159	192,395	36,764
February	-48,021	-64,018	15,997	180,613	127,828	52,785	228,635	191,847	36,788
March	-48,151	-64,480	16,328	182,528	129,205	53,323	230,679	193,685	36,994
April	-46,987	-63,629	16,642	184,174	130,340	53,833	231,161	193,969	37,192
May	-48,269	-64,992	16,723	185,036	130,947	54,089	233,305	195,939	37,366
June	-46,012	-62,746	16,734	184,726	130,588	54,138	230,738	193,334	37,404
July	-44,699	-61,268	16,569	184,436	130,415	54,021	229,135	191,683	37,452
August	-43,816	-60,429	16,613	183,949	129,818	54,131	227,765	190,247	37,519
September	-42,840	-59,648	16,808	185,071	130,666	54,405	227,911	190,314	37,598
October	-42,348	-59,722	17,374	185,018	129,885	55,133	227,365	189,607	37,759
November	-43,038	-60,881	17,844	186,165	130,347	55,817	229,202	191,228	37,974
December	-42,199	-60,492	18,293	186,521	130,104	56,417	228,720	190,595	38,124
2013									
January	-42,148	-60,835	18,687	187,843	131,094	56,749	229,991	191,929	38,062
February	-40,537	-59,435	18,898	188,424	131,668	56,756	228,961	191,103	37,857
March	-40,316	-59,187	18,870	187,470	130,868	56,602	227,787	190,055	37,732
April	-39,720	-58,375	18,655	187,565	131,092	56,473	227,285	189,468	37,818
May	-40,740	-59,263	18,523	187,291	130,725	56,565	228,031	189,989	38,042
June	-40,600	-59,028	18,428	188,445	131,663	56,782	229,045	190,690	38,354
July	-40,267	-58,782	18,515	189,158	132,164	56,994	229,425	190,946	38,479
August	-38,495	-57,174	18,679	190,291	133,001	57,290	228,786	190,174	38,612
September	-40,399	-59,312	18,913	190,252	132,696	57,556	230,651	192,008	38,643
October	-40,287	-59,219	18,932	191,608	133,800	57,808	231,895	193,019	38,876
November	-39,106	-57,965	18,859	193,047	135,108	57,940	232,153	193,073	39,080
December	-37,483	-56,363	18,881	193,897	135,701	58,196	231,380	192,064	39,316
2014									
January	-37,515	-56,939	19,424	193,399	134,841	58,558	230,914	191,780	39,134
February	-39,601	-58,788	19,186	191,016	132,713	58,303	230,617	191,500	39,117
March	-41,512	-60,779	19,268	191,396	133,179	58,217	232,907	193,958	38,949
April	-43,756	-62,823	19,067	192,010	133,691	58,320	235,767	196,513	39,253
May	-44,200	-63,755	19,555	194,939	135,879	59,060	239,139	199,634	39,505
June	-43,741	-63,104	19,363	195,525	136,238	59,287	239,266	199,342	39,924
July	-42,001	-61,096	19,095	196,763	137,562	59,201	238,764	198,658	40,105
August	-40,824	-59,992	19,168	197,489	138,260	59,228	238,312	198,252	40,060
September	-41,443	-60,690	19,247	197,333	138,045	59,288	238,776	198,735	40,041
October (R)	-41,961	-61,369	19,408	197,430	137,882	59,548	239,391	199,251	40,140
November	-41,618	-60,864	19,246	196,637	137,116	59,521	238,254	197,980	40,275
December									

(1) Data are presented on a BOP basis.

NOTES:
* The three-month moving averages shown in this exhibit are computed by summing the subject month and the two prior months, dividing by three, and showing the average at the end month of the period. A moving average is useful in smoothing the volatile trade data so that trends can better be discerned.
* For information on data sources and methodology, see the information section on page A-1 of this release or at www.census.gov/ft900 or www.bea.gov/newsreleases/international/trade/tradnewsrelease.htm.

Part A: Seasonally Adjusted (by Commodity/Service)

Exhibit 3. U.S. Services by Major Category - Exports

In millions of dollars. Details may not equal totals due to seasonal adjustment and rounding. (R) - Revised.

Period	Total Services	Maintenance and Repair Services n.i.e.	Transport	Travel (for all purposes including education) (1)	Insurance Services	Financial Services	Charges for the Use of Intellectual Property n.i.e.	Telecommuni- cations, Computer, and Information Services	Other Business Services	Government Goods and Services n.i.e.
2012										
Jan. - Dec.	654,850	15,115	83,592	161,249	16,534	76,605	125,492	32,103	119,892	24,267
Jan. - Nov.	598,018	13,762	76,364	147,400	15,144	69,892	114,633	29,280	109,405	22,138
January	52,466	1,174	6,653	12,553	1,299	6,299	10,337	2,529	9,624	1,998
February	53,439	1,203	6,899	13,020	1,308	6,431	10,379	2,546	9,634	2,019
March	54,063	1,274	7,101	13,234	1,328	6,452	10,354	2,582	9,729	2,009
April	53,998	1,229	6,986	13,489	1,360	6,161	10,262	2,637	9,907	1,968
May	54,206	1,286	7,076	13,416	1,383	6,225	10,221	2,666	9,983	1,948
June	54,211	1,268	7,095	13,573	1,398	6,067	10,232	2,671	9,958	1,949
July	53,647	1,188	6,890	13,300	1,406	6,117	10,294	2,651	9,830	1,970
August	54,536	1,185	6,926	13,799	1,412	6,292	10,401	2,665	9,853	2,003
September	55,033	1,228	6,811	13,798	1,417	6,442	10,552	2,712	10,028	2,045
October	55,830	1,358	6,915	13,393	1,421	6,747	10,748	2,792	10,353	2,102
November	56,589	1,368	7,012	13,824	1,412	6,658	10,851	2,830	10,506	2,128
December	56,833	1,353	7,228	13,849	1,391	6,713	10,860	2,823	10,487	2,129
2013										
Jan. - Dec.	687,410	16,295	87,267	173,131	16,096	84,066	129,178	33,409	123,447	24,522
Jan. - Nov.	628,821	14,727	79,687	158,311	14,735	76,697	118,566	30,640	112,854	22,603
January	56,825	1,196	7,250	14,232	1,357	6,828	10,775	2,773	10,296	2,117
February	56,610	1,131	7,350	14,254	1,333	6,792	10,735	2,752	10,165	2,099
March	56,371	1,114	7,273	14,214	1,320	6,773	10,738	2,758	10,094	2,087
April	56,437	1,126	7,253	14,093	1,316	6,912	10,786	2,793	10,084	2,073
May	56,887	1,162	7,324	14,249	1,318	7,011	10,829	2,814	10,106	2,073
June	57,023	1,239	7,302	14,294	1,326	6,936	10,868	2,820	10,161	2,077
July	57,072	1,439	7,026	14,368	1,339	6,862	10,903	2,811	10,248	2,076
August	57,777	1,528	7,116	14,801	1,349	6,870	10,880	2,800	10,326	2,107
September	57,819	1,557	7,193	14,572	1,356	7,002	10,798	2,786	10,395	2,160
October	57,829	1,618	7,235	14,562	1,359	7,329	10,658	2,770	10,456	1,842
November	58,170	1,616	7,365	14,671	1,361	7,383	10,596	2,764	10,522	1,892
December	58,590	1,568	7,580	14,820	1,360	7,369	10,612	2,769	10,593	1,919
2014										
Jan. - Nov.	649,747	16,471	81,976	163,947	15,054	81,428	123,407	30,488	115,082	21,894
January	58,914	1,449	7,513	15,229	1,343	7,171	10,825	2,707	10,562	2,116
February	57,405	1,370	7,097	14,210	1,333	6,986	10,946	2,676	10,553	2,234
March	58,332	1,404	7,427	14,690	1,332	7,027	11,014	2,675	10,548	2,217
April	59,222	1,459	7,431	14,904	1,366	7,501	11,200	2,774	10,405	2,183
May	59,626	1,517	7,629	15,137	1,387	7,606	11,284	2,829	10,333	1,904
June	59,013	1,530	7,385	14,826	1,393	7,603	11,319	2,841	10,332	1,784
July	58,962	1,517	7,424	14,908	1,386	7,390	11,306	2,810	10,401	1,821
August	59,709	1,551	7,692	15,352	1,381	7,304	11,315	2,792	10,452	1,871
September	59,194	1,507	7,512	14,827	1,378	7,418	11,347	2,787	10,485	1,932
October (R)	59,742	1,570	7,503	14,947	1,378	7,733	11,401	2,796	10,500	1,913
November	59,627	1,596	7,363	14,918	1,378	7,691	11,449	2,802	10,511	1,920
December										
October data as published last month:										
	59,493	1,570	7,521	14,864	1,378	7,549	11,401	2,796	10,500	1,913

n.i.e. Not included elsewhere

(1) All travel purposes include 1) business travel, including expenditures by border, seasonal, and other short-term workers and 2) personal travel, including health-related and education-related travel.

NOTE: For information on data sources, methodology, and definitions, see the information section on page A-1 of this release or at www.census.gov/ft900 or www.bea.gov/newsreleases/international/trade/tradnewsrelease.htm.

Part A: Seasonally Adjusted (by Commodity/Service)

Exhibit 4. U.S. Services by Major Category - Imports

In millions of dollars. Details may not equal totals due to seasonal adjustment and rounding. (R) - Revised.

Period	Total Services	Maintenance and Repair Services n.i.e.	Transport	Travel (for all purposes including education) (1)	Insurance Services	Financial Services	Charges for the Use of Intellectual Property n.i.e.	Telecommuni-cations, Computer, and Information Services	Other Business Services	Government Goods and Services n.i.e.
2012										
Jan. - Dec.	450,360	7,970	85,029	100,317	53,203	16,975	39,502	32,156	87,347	27,861
Jan. - Nov.	412,319	7,325	77,837	91,857	48,847	15,479	35,970	29,519	79,806	25,679
January	36,805	694	7,005	7,983	4,390	1,373	3,112	2,712	7,074	2,462
February	36,940	680	6,876	8,329	4,376	1,391	3,105	2,666	7,083	2,433
March	37,239	697	7,090	8,335	4,380	1,404	3,164	2,645	7,122	2,402
April	37,397	684	7,115	8,328	4,403	1,374	3,286	2,649	7,190	2,368
May	37,462	687	7,055	8,388	4,427	1,383	3,294	2,661	7,226	2,341
June	37,353	678	7,080	8,357	4,453	1,367	3,186	2,680	7,230	2,322
July	37,542	641	7,223	8,351	4,480	1,361	3,266	2,706	7,202	2,311
August	37,661	644	6,986	8,271	4,496	1,367	3,643	2,718	7,241	2,295
September	37,591	629	7,162	8,479	4,501	1,438	3,047	2,714	7,345	2,275
October	38,025	642	7,066	8,495	4,494	1,514	3,353	2,696	7,515	2,250
November	38,306	648	7,179	8,541	4,446	1,507	3,514	2,671	7,580	2,219
December	38,042	645	7,192	8,460	4,355	1,496	3,532	2,638	7,541	2,182
2013										
Jan. - Dec.	462,134	7,620	90,754	104,677	50,454	18,683	39,015	32,877	92,710	25,343
Jan. - Nov.	422,734	7,022	83,006	95,659	46,389	17,001	35,707	30,063	84,600	23,288
January	37,838	627	7,459	8,510	4,223	1,479	3,406	2,597	7,397	2,139
February	37,693	614	7,602	8,518	4,149	1,433	3,321	2,601	7,340	2,115
March	37,665	628	7,396	8,636	4,135	1,466	3,275	2,647	7,370	2,111
April	38,096	644	7,453	8,676	4,180	1,523	3,270	2,737	7,487	2,126
May	38,366	659	7,497	8,658	4,226	1,560	3,246	2,787	7,598	2,134
June	38,602	657	7,527	8,768	4,274	1,537	3,204	2,798	7,702	2,135
July	38,470	667	7,459	8,657	4,323	1,524	3,143	2,769	7,799	2,129
August	38,765	668	7,543	8,827	4,323	1,513	3,130	2,759	7,882	2,120
September	38,695	658	7,519	8,662	4,274	1,588	3,165	2,767	7,953	2,108
October	39,170	603	7,685	8,886	4,176	1,674	3,249	2,793	8,010	2,094
November	39,377	596	7,866	8,862	4,106	1,702	3,297	2,808	8,062	2,077
December	39,400	598	7,748	9,018	4,066	1,682	3,308	2,814	8,110	2,056
2014										
Jan. - Nov.	437,470	7,179	86,030	101,779	44,383	17,692	37,858	30,607	89,889	22,053
January	38,626	598	7,603	8,708	4,021	1,591	3,255	2,772	8,042	2,036
February	39,324	606	7,627	8,784	3,986	1,498	4,012	2,753	8,044	2,014
March	38,898	616	7,821	8,905	3,959	1,526	3,247	2,751	8,065	2,007
April	39,538	656	7,802	9,231	4,078	1,583	3,340	2,756	8,049	2,043
May	40,081	664	7,896	9,502	4,132	1,621	3,386	2,765	8,064	2,051
June	40,153	677	7,771	9,479	4,122	1,645	3,535	2,778	8,111	2,037
July	40,081	680	7,784	9,502	4,048	1,609	3,478	2,794	8,189	1,998
August	39,945	668	7,835	9,426	4,005	1,593	3,382	2,805	8,257	1,973
September	40,096	675	7,926	9,375	3,994	1,650	3,389	2,811	8,314	1,962
October (R)	40,378	665	8,003	9,468	4,013	1,683	3,406	2,811	8,362	1,966
November	40,350	673	7,962	9,397	4,025	1,692	3,429	2,811	8,393	1,967
December										
October data as published last month:	40,253	666	8,011	9,354	4,013	1,664	3,406	2,811	8,362	1,966

n.i.e. Not included elsewhere

(1) All travel purposes include 1) business travel, including expenditures by border, seasonal, and other short-term workers and 2) personal travel, including health-related and education-related travel.

NOTE: For information on data sources, methodology, and definitions, see the information section on page A-1 of this release or at www.census.gov/ft900 or www.bea.gov/newsreleases/international/trade/tradnewsrelease.htm.

Part A: Seasonally Adjusted (by Commodity/Service)

Exhibit 5. U.S. Trade in Goods

In millions of dollars. Details may not equal totals due to seasonal adjustment and rounding. (R) - Revised.

Period	Balance		Exports			Imports		
	Total Balance of Payments Basis	Total Census Basis	Total Balance of Payments Basis	Net Adjustments	Total Census Basis	Total Balance of Payments Basis	Net Adjustments	Total Census Basis
2012								
Jan. - Dec.	-742,095	-730,599	1,561,689	15,986	1,545,703	2,303,785	27,482	2,276,302
Jan. - Nov.	-685,671	-675,126	1,428,757	14,794	1,413,964	2,114,428	25,338	2,089,090
January	-66,927	-65,813	127,140	1,404	125,736	194,068	2,519	191,549
February	-59,838	-59,065	128,281	1,509	126,772	188,119	2,281	185,837
March	-66,673	-65,561	132,195	1,283	130,912	198,868	2,396	196,472
April	-64,375	-63,647	130,545	1,532	129,013	194,920	2,260	192,660
May	-63,928	-62,772	130,100	1,110	128,990	194,028	2,266	191,762
June	-59,936	-58,941	131,119	1,293	129,826	191,055	2,288	188,767
July	-59,939	-59,227	130,026	1,525	128,501	189,965	2,238	187,727
August	-61,411	-60,532	128,309	1,398	126,911	189,720	2,277	187,443
September	-57,593	-56,648	133,663	1,337	132,325	191,256	2,282	188,974
October	-60,163	-59,019	127,682	1,181	126,501	187,845	2,325	185,520
November	-64,888	-63,902	129,697	1,221	128,476	194,585	2,207	192,378
December	-56,424	-55,473	132,932	1,193	131,739	189,357	2,145	187,212
2013								
Jan. - Dec.	-701,669	-688,728	1,592,784	13,191	1,579,593	2,294,453	26,131	2,268,321
Jan. - Nov.	-645,086	-633,471	1,458,574	12,123	1,446,452	2,103,660	23,738	2,079,922
January	-61,192	-60,576	130,653	1,494	129,159	191,846	2,111	189,735
February	-60,688	-59,282	131,420	932	130,488	192,107	2,338	189,769
March	-55,680	-54,742	130,532	1,193	129,339	186,211	2,130	184,081
April	-58,758	-57,638	131,326	1,003	130,323	190,084	2,123	187,962
May	-63,352	-62,293	130,319	963	129,356	193,671	2,022	191,648
June	-54,973	-53,568	133,343	632	132,711	188,316	2,037	186,279
July	-58,021	-57,021	132,830	1,173	131,657	190,851	2,174	188,677
August	-58,527	-57,606	132,829	1,305	131,524	191,356	2,227	189,129
September	-61,387	-60,416	132,430	1,147	131,282	193,817	2,118	191,699
October	-57,742	-56,483	136,141	926	135,215	193,884	2,185	191,698
November	-54,765	-53,845	136,752	1,354	135,398	191,517	2,274	189,243
December	-56,583	-55,258	134,210	1,068	133,141	190,792	2,393	188,399
2014								
Jan. - Nov.	-673,612	-660,868	1,497,694	11,264	1,486,430	2,171,307	24,008	2,147,298
January	-59,469	-58,798	133,561	1,593	131,968	193,029	2,264	190,766
February	-60,311	-58,106	130,367	188	130,179	190,679	2,394	188,285
March	-62,558	-61,256	135,608	1,178	134,431	198,166	2,479	195,687
April	-65,599	-64,674	135,096	1,204	133,892	200,695	2,129	198,566
May	-63,107	-62,238	136,933	1,266	135,667	200,040	2,135	197,905
June	-60,605	-59,634	136,685	1,154	135,531	197,290	2,125	195,165
July	-59,576	-58,733	139,069	1,300	137,769	198,645	2,143	196,502
August	-59,795	-58,587	139,027	819	138,208	198,822	2,027	196,795
September	-62,700	-61,307	136,038	745	135,294	198,739	2,138	196,600
October (R)	-61,613	-60,402	138,580	876	137,704	200,192	2,087	198,105
November	-58,279	-57,133	136,730	942	135,789	195,009	2,087	192,922
December								
October data as published last month:								
	-62,671	-61,397	138,045	814	137,231	200,716	2,088	198,628

NOTE: For information on data sources, nonsampling errors, definitions and details concerning what is included in the Net Adjustments, see the information section on page A-1 of this release or at www.census.gov/ft900 or www.bea.gov/newsreleases/international/trade/tradnewsrelease.htm.

Exhibit 6. Exports and Imports of Goods by Principal End-Use Category

In millions of dollars. Details may not equal totals due to seasonal adjustment and rounding. (R) - Revised.

Period	Total Balance of Payments Basis	Net Adjustments	Total Census Basis (1)	End-Use Commodity Category					
				Foods, Feeds, & Beverages	Industrial Supplies (2)	Capital Goods	Automotive Vehicles, etc.	Consumer Goods	Other Goods
Exports									
2013									
Jan. - Dec.	1,592,784	13,191	1,579,593	136,184	509,313	534,205	152,556	189,090	58,245
Jan. - Nov.	1,458,574	12,123	1,446,452	123,474	466,031	489,746	140,043	173,721	53,436
January	130,653	1,494	129,159	11,520	41,261	44,099	12,228	15,649	4,402
February	131,420	932	130,488	11,590	43,048	43,244	12,417	15,161	5,026
March	130,532	1,193	129,339	10,792	42,627	43,511	12,281	14,911	5,216
April	131,326	1,003	130,323	10,384	41,710	44,195	12,699	16,732	4,602
May	130,319	963	129,356	10,227	40,789	44,876	12,978	15,609	4,876
June	133,343	632	132,711	10,580	42,331	45,628	12,650	16,447	5,076
July	132,830	1,173	131,657	10,805	43,326	44,570	12,518	15,767	4,672
August	132,829	1,305	131,524	10,471	42,855	44,689	13,063	15,629	4,818
September	132,430	1,147	131,282	12,017	41,348	44,590	13,130	15,645	4,553
October	136,141	926	135,215	12,527	43,380	45,076	13,017	16,359	4,856
November	136,752	1,354	135,398	12,560	43,356	45,268	13,063	15,812	5,339
December	134,210	1,068	133,141	12,710	43,282	44,458	12,513	15,369	4,809
2014									
Jan. - Nov.	1,497,694	11,264	1,486,430	128,361	467,305	503,824	146,339	182,713	57,888
January	133,561	1,593	131,968	11,787	43,604	44,491	12,205	15,420	4,462
February	130,367	188	130,179	11,825	40,793	43,845	12,180	16,674	4,862
March	135,608	1,178	134,431	12,153	41,781	46,114	12,886	16,413	5,084
April	135,096	1,204	133,892	11,893	41,979	45,808	12,717	16,337	5,158
May	136,933	1,266	135,667	11,965	42,181	45,644	13,491	16,747	5,638
June	136,685	1,154	135,531	11,693	42,206	45,670	13,655	17,157	5,149
July	139,069	1,300	137,769	11,061	43,495	46,124	15,312	16,509	5,266
August	139,027	819	138,208	10,518	44,232	47,112	13,591	17,273	5,482
September	136,038	745	135,294	11,787	42,163	45,943	13,488	16,587	5,326
October (R)	138,580	876	137,704	11,703	42,081	47,687	13,652	17,024	5,557
November	136,730	942	135,789	11,977	42,789	45,387	13,162	16,571	5,902
December									
Imports									
2013									
Jan. - Dec.	2,294,453	26,131	2,268,321	115,146	681,576	554,518	308,802	532,743	75,537
Jan. - Nov.	2,103,660	23,738	2,079,922	105,616	627,126	507,517	282,488	487,757	69,417
January	191,846	2,111	189,735	9,269	60,339	45,937	24,045	44,038	6,108
February	192,107	2,338	189,769	9,587	58,510	46,189	24,664	44,913	5,906
March	186,211	2,130	184,081	9,516	56,989	44,648	24,584	41,908	6,437
April	190,084	2,123	187,962	9,599	56,733	45,483	25,219	44,313	6,615
May	193,671	2,022	191,648	9,839	57,457	45,695	26,097	45,496	7,065
June	188,316	2,037	186,279	9,595	55,175	46,006	25,598	43,716	6,190
July	190,851	2,174	188,677	9,579	56,509	45,625	26,082	44,468	6,415
August	191,356	2,227	189,129	9,629	56,560	46,752	26,117	43,826	6,245
September	193,817	2,118	191,699	9,605	57,217	46,904	26,784	45,017	6,172
October	193,884	2,185	191,698	9,786	57,231	46,879	26,243	45,055	6,504
November	191,517	2,274	189,243	9,612	54,406	47,399	27,055	45,009	5,762
December	190,792	2,393	188,399	9,529	54,450	47,001	26,315	44,986	6,119
2014									
Jan. - Nov.	2,171,307	24,008	2,147,298	115,376	612,437	540,540	299,598	508,704	70,643
January	193,029	2,264	190,766	9,711	57,456	47,683	25,438	44,647	5,831
February	190,679	2,394	188,285	9,548	57,257	46,470	25,562	43,532	5,915
March	198,166	2,479	195,687	10,590	58,003	47,797	26,280	46,387	6,629
April	200,695	2,129	198,566	10,752	57,688	48,631	27,166	47,400	6,928
May	200,040	2,135	197,905	10,598	55,816	49,622	28,540	47,072	6,257
June	197,290	2,125	195,165	10,830	55,437	49,449	27,485	45,624	6,339
July	198,645	2,143	196,502	10,833	55,767	49,093	28,922	45,093	6,795
August	198,822	2,027	196,795	10,540	55,635	50,880	27,528	45,788	6,424
September	198,739	2,138	196,600	10,684	54,588	49,916	26,981	47,701	6,730
October (R)	200,192	2,087	198,105	10,891	54,700	50,897	28,220	46,929	6,468
November	195,009	2,087	192,922	10,396	50,091	50,100	27,475	48,531	6,328
December									

(1) Detailed data are presented on a Census basis. The information needed to convert to a BOP basis is not available.
(2) Includes petroleum and petroleum products.

NOTE: For information on data sources, nonsampling errors and definitions, see the information section on page A-1 of this release or at www.census.gov/ft900 or www.bea.gov/newsreleases/international/trade/tradnewsrelease.htm.

Part A: Seasonally Adjusted (by Commodity/Service)

Exhibit 7. Exports of Goods by End-Use Category and Commodity

In millions of dollars. Details may not equal totals due to seasonal adjustment and rounding. The commodities in this exhibit are ranked on the monthly change within each major commodity grouping. (-) Represents zero or less than one-half of measurement shown. (R) - Revised.

Item (1)	November 2014	October 2014 (R)	Monthly Change	Year-to-Date 2014	Year-to-Date 2013	Year-to-Date Change
Total, Balance of Payments Basis	136,730	138,580	-1,849	1,497,694	1,458,574	39,120
Net Adjustments	942	876	65	11,264	12,123	-858
Total, Census Basis	135,789	137,704	-1,915	1,486,430	1,446,452	39,978
Foods, feeds, and beverages	11,977	11,703	274	128,361	123,474	4,887
Soybeans	2,824	2,160	664	18,803	19,868	-1,066
Rice	235	163	72	2,016	2,062	-47
Sorghum, barley, oats	166	130	35	1,635	590	1,045
Wheat	558	523	35	7,214	9,886	-2,672
Oilseeds, food oils	254	228	25	2,616	2,727	-111
Other foods	1,110	1,113	-3	12,144	11,770	374
Fish and shellfish	503	509	-6	5,509	5,340	169
Nonagricultural foods, etc.	134	141	-6	1,535	1,568	-33
Dairy products and eggs	432	439	-8	5,794	5,227	567
Alcoholic beverages, excluding wine	155	170	-14	1,876	1,776	100
Bakery products	526	549	-23	5,913	5,946	-33
Wine, beer, and related products	151	176	-24	1,938	1,964	-26
Meat, poultry, etc.	1,641	1,666	-25	18,420	16,916	1,504
Fruits, frozen juices	776	806	-30	8,633	8,676	-42
Vegetables	541	581	-39	6,416	6,203	213
Animal feeds, n.e.c.	660	707	-46	8,250	8,183	67
Nuts	682	771	-88	8,169	7,823	346
Corn	627	871	-244	11,482	6,950	4,532
Industrial supplies and materials	42,789	42,081	708	467,305	466,031	1,273
Fuel oil	4,603	4,020	583	56,509	58,602	-2,093
Nonmonetary gold	2,914	2,554	360	20,784	32,677	-11,894
Petroleum products, other	5,097	4,878	219	58,278	54,587	3,691
Crude oil	1,152	960	192	10,613	4,217	6,395
Nonferrous metals, other	728	595	133	7,455	6,403	1,052
Chemicals-organic	2,866	2,787	79	30,127	32,133	-2,006
Copper	853	786	66	7,999	7,855	144
Chemicals-other	2,721	2,657	64	28,402	27,833	569
Coal and fuels, other	464	415	49	5,347	5,967	-620
Nuclear fuel materials	150	103	47	905	1,189	-285
Plastic materials	3,119	3,081	38	33,882	33,296	586
Cotton, raw	331	306	26	3,842	5,178	-1,337
Shingles, molding, wallboard	448	425	23	4,536	4,335	201
Other industrial supplies	2,234	2,217	17	23,816	22,683	1,133
Nontextile floor tiles	63	47	16	576	544	32
Hides and skins	229	216	12	2,694	2,890	-196
Finished textile supplies	270	259	11	2,966	2,772	193
Tobacco, unmanufactured	76	66	10	1,008	1,106	-98
Glass-plate, sheet, etc.	155	145	10	1,473	1,523	-50
Pulpwood and woodpulp	774	766	8	8,358	8,333	25
Logs and lumber	557	551	5	6,332	5,754	578
Industrial rubber products	447	442	4	4,855	4,596	259
Tapes, audio and visual	23	22	1	216	257	-41
Manmade cloth	635	634	1	6,757	6,679	78
Hair, waste materials	55	57	-2	605	605	(-)
Cotton fiber cloth	215	217	-3	2,308	2,285	23
Electric energy	21	24	-3	563	303	259
Mineral supplies-manufactured	501	506	-5	5,412	5,109	303
Wood supplies, manufactured	115	125	-10	1,321	1,297	24
Iron and steel mill products	944	954	-11	10,333	10,247	86
Leather and furs	126	137	-11	1,303	1,155	147
Agric. farming-unmanufactured	213	229	-15	3,082	3,080	2
Agriculture-manufactured, other	241	258	-17	2,774	2,590	184
Nonmetallic minerals	76	94	-19	932	786	146
Gas-natural	434	460	-26	7,302	5,717	1,585
Agric. industry-unmanufactured	280	308	-28	4,686	4,554	131
Synthetic rubber-primary	315	345	-30	3,634	3,692	-58
Iron and steel products, other	620	651	-31	6,991	6,757	234
Chemicals-inorganic	764	801	-37	8,433	8,380	53
Newsprint	1,107	1,148	-42	12,331	12,310	22
Aluminum and alumina	731	795	-64	8,164	8,632	-469
Chemicals-fertilizers	797	873	-77	8,707	8,797	-90
Precious metals, other	553	652	-99	6,914	6,887	27
Metallurgical grade coal	450	557	-107	5,829	7,232	-1,404
Steelmaking materials	833	947	-114	8,748	9,659	-910
Finished metal shapes	1,717	1,885	-169	19,262	18,468	794
Natural gas liquids	777	1,123	-346	9,940	6,075	3,866

Part A: Seasonally Adjusted (by Commodity/Service)

Exhibit 7. Exports of Goods by End-Use Category and Commodity

In millions of dollars. Details may not equal totals due to seasonal adjustment and rounding. The commodities in this exhibit are ranked on the monthly change within each major commodity grouping. (-) Represents zero or less than one-half of measurement shown. (R) - Revised.

Item (1)	November 2014	October 2014 (R)	Monthly Change	Year-to-Date 2014	Year-to-Date 2013	Year-to-Date Change
Capital goods, except automotive	**45,387**	**47,687**	**-2,299**	**503,824**	**489,746**	**14,078**
Civilian aircraft	4,601	5,703	-1,103	52,741	49,274	3,468
Generators, accessories	1,203	1,506	-303	13,451	13,135	316
Computer accessories	2,467	2,607	-139	29,379	28,776	604
Computers	1,339	1,466	-126	15,551	15,302	248
Excavating machinery	1,016	1,141	-125	12,064	13,704	-1,640
Railway transportation equipment	389	509	-120	3,888	3,754	134
Agricultural machinery, equipment	581	688	-107	7,851	8,499	-649
Engines-civilian aircraft	2,879	2,974	-95	29,739	27,198	2,540
Materials handling equipment	1,094	1,187	-93	13,276	14,083	-807
Vessels, excluding scrap	5	96	-90	350	98	252
Industrial machines, other	4,650	4,718	-68	49,722	44,549	5,172
Parts-civilian aircraft	1,787	1,820	-33	20,535	19,817	718
Photo, service industry machinery	894	925	-32	9,931	10,199	-268
Pulp and paper machinery	204	235	-30	2,341	2,268	73
Measuring, testing, control instruments	2,070	2,095	-25	23,087	22,681	407
Semiconductors	3,523	3,547	-25	39,641	38,989	652
Nonfarm tractors and parts	203	225	-23	2,824	2,844	-19
Telecommunications equipment	3,373	3,396	-23	36,875	36,318	557
Business machines and equipment	242	264	-22	2,736	2,741	-6
Spacecraft, excluding military	3	20	-17	77	57	20
Specialized mining	159	174	-15	1,462	1,634	-172
Marine engines, parts	123	137	-14	1,316	1,352	-36
Commercial vessels, other	38	38	(-)	539	570	-31
Medicinal equipment	2,886	2,880	5	32,158	31,383	775
Metalworking machine tools	643	637	6	6,884	7,095	-211
Textile, sewing machines	109	101	8	1,092	1,078	14
Laboratory testing instruments	946	936	9	10,277	10,045	232
Electric apparatus	3,630	3,611	19	38,896	36,898	1,998
Wood, glass, plastic	360	329	31	3,698	3,756	-57
Food, tobacco machinery	374	329	45	3,675	3,523	151
Drilling & oilfield equipment	1,107	1,007	99	10,861	11,294	-433
Industrial engines	2,493	2,386	107	26,910	26,834	77
Automotive vehicles, parts, and engines	**13,162**	**13,652**	**-490**	**146,339**	**140,043**	**6,296**
Consumer goods	**16,571**	**17,024**	**-453**	**182,713**	**173,721**	**8,993**
Jewelry, etc.	842	1,069	-227	11,843	10,781	1,062
Artwork, antiques, stamps, etc.	791	925	-134	9,535	7,274	2,261
Toys, games, and sporting goods	821	897	-76	9,549	9,404	144
Pharmaceutical preparations	4,364	4,435	-71	46,698	44,626	2,072
Televisions and video equipment	404	453	-49	4,214	4,057	157
Furniture, household goods, etc.	411	434	-22	4,690	4,514	176
Books, printed matter	414	431	-16	4,665	4,918	-253
Pleasure boats and motors	228	243	-16	2,251	2,247	4
Other consumer nondurables	622	635	-13	6,917	6,979	-62
Recorded media	215	221	-6	2,454	2,850	-397
Stereo equipment, etc.	167	173	-6	1,968	1,863	105
Cookware, cutlery, tools	98	103	-5	1,081	999	82
Glassware, chinaware	50	54	-4	550	523	27
Tobacco, manufactured	50	54	-4	575	629	-54
Musical instruments	164	165	-2	1,891	2,001	-111
Rugs	91	92	(-)	1,025	1,028	-3
Nursery stock, etc.	36	36	(-)	388	386	2
Apparel, household goods-nontextile	261	259	2	2,757	2,760	-4
Household appliances	655	653	2	6,911	6,892	20
Sports apparel and gear	70	66	4	765	673	92
Toiletries and cosmetics	1,023	1,006	17	10,803	10,384	419
Apparel, household goods-textile	640	623	17	6,511	6,290	221
Cell phones and other household goods, n.e.c.	2,139	2,106	33	22,603	21,407	1,196
Numismatic coins	100	64	36	876	983	-108
Gem diamonds	1,916	1,829	87	21,195	19,252	1,943
Other goods	**5,902**	**5,557**	**345**	**57,888**	**53,436**	**4,452**

(1) Detailed data are presented on a Census basis. The information needed to convert to a BOP basis is not available.

NOTE: For information on data sources, nonsampling errors and definitions, see the information section on page A-1 of this release or at www.census.gov/ft900 or www.bea.gov/newsreleases/international/trade/tradnewsrelease.htm.

Part A: Seasonally Adjusted (by Commodity/Service)

Exhibit 8. Imports of Goods by End-Use Category and Commodity

In millions of dollars. Details may not equal totals due to seasonal adjustment and rounding. The commodities in this exhibit are ranked on the monthly change within each major commodity grouping. (-) Represents zero or less than one-half of measurement shown. (R) - Revised.

Item (1)	November 2014	October 2014 (R)	Monthly Change	Year-to-Date 2014	Year-to-Date 2013	Year-to-Date Change
Total, Balance of Payments Basis	**195,009**	**200,192**	**-5,184**	**2,171,307**	**2,103,660**	**67,646**
Net Adjustments	2,087	2,087	-1	24,008	23,738	270
Total, Census Basis	**192,922**	**198,105**	**-5,183**	**2,147,298**	**2,079,922**	**67,376**
Foods, feeds, and beverages	**10,396**	**10,891**	**-495**	**115,376**	**105,616**	**9,759**
Food oils, oilseeds	437	558	-120	6,463	5,845	618
Other foods	1,034	1,109	-75	11,675	11,204	471
Cane and beet sugar	72	144	-72	1,499	1,506	-7
Green coffee	449	520	-71	4,933	4,354	579
Fruits, frozen juices	1,186	1,255	-69	13,185	12,073	1,112
Feedstuff and foodgrains	489	523	-34	6,092	6,419	-327
Dairy products and eggs	153	185	-32	1,784	1,618	166
Cocoa beans	47	67	-20	1,202	957	246
Vegetables	937	955	-19	9,962	9,842	119
Tea, spices, etc.	178	192	-14	1,950	1,820	131
Alcoholic beverages, excluding wine	582	595	-13	6,471	6,378	93
Fish and shellfish	1,675	1,681	-6	18,754	16,348	2,406
Bakery products	784	790	-6	8,535	8,235	300
Nuts	219	220	-1	2,135	1,835	300
Wine, beer, and related products	789	785	3	8,939	8,386	553
Nonagricultural foods, etc.	103	84	19	951	765	186
Meat products	1,261	1,228	33	10,844	8,031	2,813
Industrial supplies and materials	**50,091**	**54,700**	**-4,609**	**612,437**	**627,126**	**-14,688**
Crude oil	17,089	19,291	-2,202	228,389	251,321	-22,932
Fuel oil	2,460	3,160	-700	37,300	41,415	-4,115
Iron and steel mill products	2,199	2,592	-393	23,385	16,524	6,861
Nonmonetary gold	896	1,152	-256	13,086	14,742	-1,656
Petroleum products, other	3,199	3,408	-209	39,522	44,371	-4,849
Copper	353	472	-119	4,645	5,826	-1,181
Plastic materials	1,440	1,556	-116	15,774	14,076	1,699
Chemicals-fertilizers	1,212	1,323	-111	13,949	14,474	-525
Steelmaking materials	633	739	-106	8,064	6,726	1,338
Bauxite and aluminum	1,057	1,151	-94	10,419	9,542	876
Nuclear fuel materials	244	333	-90	3,179	4,091	-912
Industrial supplies, other	2,597	2,680	-83	28,391	26,726	1,665
Finished metal shapes	1,432	1,507	-76	16,164	15,399	764
Chemicals-other, n.e.c.	1,020	1,083	-63	11,559	10,870	689
Tobacco, waxes, etc.	803	863	-60	8,353	8,179	174
Nickel	227	282	-55	2,767	2,180	588
Paper and paper products	611	649	-38	6,835	6,503	332
Lumber	507	543	-36	5,373	4,738	635
Chemicals-inorganic	591	625	-34	6,871	6,776	96
Stone, sand, cement, etc.	438	466	-28	4,680	4,265	415
Pulpwood and woodpulp	249	274	-25	3,274	3,320	-45
Iron and steel, advanced	843	867	-24	9,102	8,396	706
Finished textile supplies	395	406	-11	4,314	4,052	262
Liquefied petroleum gases	318	327	-9	3,702	3,701	1
Glass-plate, sheet, etc.	139	144	-5	1,441	1,225	216
Electric energy	186	191	-5	2,494	2,221	272
Newsprint	100	104	-5	1,220	1,187	33
Shingles, wallboard	827	832	-4	8,635	8,227	408
Zinc	145	147	-2	1,480	1,366	114
Tin	71	73	-2	822	800	21
Cotton cloth, fabrics	105	106	-2	1,088	1,128	-40
Sulfur, nonmetallic minerals	117	119	-2	1,273	1,322	-49
Synthetic rubber-primary	239	240	-1	2,743	2,590	153
Cotton, natural fibers	5	6	-1	70	65	5
Hides and skins	42	42	-1	367	262	105
Iron and steel products, n.e.c.	884	884	(-)	9,295	8,542	753
Wool, silk, etc.	65	65	(-)	732	668	64
Nontextile floor tiles	282	279	3	2,898	2,624	274
Hair, waste materials	90	86	4	925	844	81
Leather and furs	66	62	5	702	627	75
Nonferrous metals, other	388	383	5	4,219	3,843	377
Plywood and veneers	223	217	6	2,442	2,223	219
Blank tapes, audio & visual	50	43	7	591	713	-123
Natural rubber	143	136	7	1,807	2,353	-546
Farming materials, livestock	140	132	7	1,708	1,843	-135
Synthetic cloth	551	540	11	5,764	5,560	204
Materials, excluding chemicals	145	119	25	1,390	1,296	94
Other precious metals	907	865	43	9,933	10,922	-988
Chemicals-organic	2,213	2,153	60	26,039	24,327	1,713
Coal and related fuels	251	167	84	1,921	2,980	-1,058
Gas-natural	907	814	93	11,343	9,156	2,187

Part A: Seasonally Adjusted (by Commodity/Service)

Exhibit 8. Imports of Goods by End-Use Category and Commodity

In millions of dollars. Details may not equal totals due to seasonal adjustment and rounding. The commodities in this exhibit are ranked on the monthly change within each major commodity grouping. (-) Represents zero or less than one-half of measurement shown. (R) - Revised.

Item (1)	November 2014	October 2014 (R)	Monthly Change	Year-to-Date 2014	Year-to-Date 2013	Year-to-Date Change
Capital goods, except automotive	**50,100**	**50,897**	**-796**	**540,540**	**507,517**	**33,022**
Computers	5,756	6,119	-363	58,298	59,129	-831
Semiconductors	3,694	3,892	-199	40,016	37,953	2,063
Industrial machines, other	4,383	4,490	-107	49,395	43,340	6,055
Photo, service industry machinery	1,474	1,559	-84	15,935	15,003	932
Parts-civilian aircraft	1,444	1,526	-82	16,157	14,003	2,154
Metalworking machine tools	945	1,023	-77	10,457	10,428	29
Materials handling equipment	1,239	1,310	-70	13,846	12,493	1,353
Telecommunications equipment	4,808	4,860	-52	53,581	50,068	3,513
Agricultural machinery, equipment	797	845	-48	9,544	9,104	440
Electric apparatus	4,095	4,130	-35	44,304	41,743	2,560
Engines-civilian aircraft	1,605	1,638	-32	17,241	15,973	1,268
Railway transportation equipment	126	157	-31	1,496	1,285	211
Measuring, testing, control instruments	1,704	1,735	-31	18,296	17,176	1,120
Excavating machinery	1,026	1,051	-26	10,186	9,476	710
Business machines and equipment	389	409	-19	4,416	4,221	195
Specialized mining	47	65	-18	645	649	-4
Spacecraft, excluding military	25	41	-16	172	131	41
Pulp and paper machinery	390	401	-11	4,254	3,887	367
Marine engines, parts	89	96	-7	1,052	1,048	3
Vessels, except scrap	(-)	(-)	(-)	15	11	4
Generators, accessories	1,900	1,900	1	20,787	19,419	1,368
Commercial vessels, other	10	7	2	148	144	4
Nonfarm tractors and parts	186	173	13	2,143	2,078	65
Industrial engines	2,086	2,072	14	22,597	20,181	2,416
Laboratory testing instruments	476	461	15	5,266	4,939	327
Drilling & oilfield equipment	863	847	16	8,860	8,399	461
Food, tobacco machinery	316	297	19	3,279	3,086	193
Textile, sewing machines	196	175	20	1,996	1,869	128
Wood, glass, plastic	600	569	30	6,649	6,340	309
Medicinal equipment	2,972	2,891	81	31,466	29,755	1,711
Computer accessories	5,068	4,948	120	52,421	51,494	926
Civilian aircraft	1,389	1,210	179	15,623	12,693	2,929
Automotive vehicles, parts, and engines	**27,475**	**28,220**	**-745**	**299,598**	**282,488**	**17,110**
Consumer goods	**48,531**	**46,929**	**1,602**	**508,704**	**487,757**	**20,947**
Cell phones and other household goods, n.e.c.	9,683	7,808	1,875	86,020	82,439	3,582
Jewelry	1,309	1,060	249	12,261	11,752	509
Gem diamonds	2,184	2,042	143	22,434	21,308	1,126
Apparel, textiles, nonwool or cotton	3,913	3,844	69	41,171	38,125	3,045
Household appliances	2,288	2,219	69	23,062	21,302	1,759
Pleasure boats and motors	240	198	42	2,426	2,218	208
Televisions and video equipment	2,322	2,300	22	26,077	26,616	-539
Apparel, household goods-nontextile	808	790	18	8,530	8,199	331
Photo equipment	315	299	16	3,169	3,592	-423
Books, printed matter	328	316	11	3,431	3,342	89
Musical instruments	145	133	11	1,557	1,469	88
Motorcycles and parts	246	240	6	2,688	2,804	-116
Nursery stock, etc.	143	138	6	1,577	1,540	36
Recorded media	65	61	4	691	765	-74
Rugs	208	208	(-)	2,252	1,989	263
Glassware, chinaware	196	196	(-)	2,165	2,059	106
Other consumer nondurables	1,207	1,215	-8	13,251	12,742	509
Apparel, household goods-wool	300	308	-8	3,269	2,921	347
Toys, games, and sporting goods	2,820	2,829	-9	31,317	30,364	953
Gem stones, other	306	316	-10	3,309	3,156	154
Cookware, cutlery, tools	728	738	-11	7,914	7,658	256
Furniture, household goods, etc.	2,641	2,654	-12	27,375	25,094	2,281
Numismatic coins	154	172	-18	1,671	2,440	-769
Toiletries and cosmetics	854	874	-20	9,336	8,752	584
Stereo equipment, etc	494	529	-35	6,264	6,254	10
Footwear	1,692	1,775	-83	18,609	17,832	778
Camping apparel and gear	850	973	-123	9,424	8,705	718
Pharmaceutical preparations	7,491	7,669	-178	83,881	77,869	6,012
Apparel, household goods-cotton	3,834	4,041	-208	43,410	44,570	-1,160
Artwork, antiques, stamps, etc.	767	983	-216	10,164	9,881	283
Other goods	**6,328**	**6,468**	**-140**	**70,643**	**69,417**	**1,225**

(1) Detailed data are presented on a Census basis. The information needed to convert to a BOP basis is not available.

NOTE: For information on data sources, nonsampling errors and definitions, see the information section on page A-1 of this release or at www.census.gov/ft900 or www.bea.gov/newsreleases/international/trade/tradnewsrelease.htm.

Part A: Seasonally Adjusted (by Commodity/Service)

Exhibit 9. Exports, Imports, and Balance of Goods, Petroleum and Non-Petroleum End-Use Category Totals

In millions of dollars. Details may not equal totals due to seasonal adjustment and rounding. (R) - Revised.

Period	Balance				Exports				Imports			
	Total	Net Adjust-ments	Petroleum (1)	Non-petroleum	Total	Net Adjust-ments	Petroleum (1)	Non-petroleum	Total	Net Adjust-ments	Petroleum (1)	Non-petroleum
2013												
Jan. - Dec.	-701,669	-12,940	-232,132	-456,596	1,592,784	13,191	137,558	1,442,035	2,294,453	26,131	369,690	1,898,631
Jan. - Nov.	-645,086	-11,615	-217,327	-416,144	1,458,574	12,123	123,481	1,322,970	2,103,660	23,738	340,808	1,739,114
January	-61,192	-616	-24,011	-36,566	130,653	1,494	9,437	119,722	191,846	2,111	33,447	156,288
February	-60,688	-1,406	-21,150	-38,132	131,420	932	10,810	119,677	192,107	2,338	31,960	157,810
March	-55,680	-937	-20,868	-33,874	130,532	1,193	9,717	119,622	186,211	2,130	30,586	153,496
April	-58,758	-1,120	-20,740	-36,898	131,326	1,003	9,854	120,469	190,084	2,123	30,594	157,368
May	-63,352	-1,059	-20,996	-41,296	130,319	963	10,262	119,094	193,671	2,022	31,258	160,390
June	-54,973	-1,405	-17,931	-35,637	133,343	632	11,476	121,236	188,316	2,037	29,407	156,873
July	-58,021	-1,001	-18,990	-38,031	132,830	1,173	12,093	119,563	190,851	2,174	31,083	157,594
August	-58,527	-922	-18,684	-38,921	132,829	1,305	12,251	119,273	191,356	2,227	30,935	158,194
September	-61,387	-971	-19,634	-40,782	132,430	1,147	11,789	119,494	193,817	2,118	31,423	160,276
October	-57,742	-1,259	-18,578	-37,905	136,141	926	12,702	122,513	193,884	2,185	31,280	160,418
November	-54,765	-920	-15,744	-38,102	136,752	1,354	13,091	122,307	191,517	2,274	28,835	160,409
December	-56,583	-1,325	-14,805	-40,452	134,210	1,068	14,077	119,065	190,792	2,393	28,882	159,517
2014												
Jan. - Nov.	-673,612	-12,744	-173,572	-487,296	1,497,694	11,264	135,340	1,351,089	2,171,307	24,008	308,912	1,838,386
January	-59,469	-671	-18,789	-40,009	133,561	1,593	12,239	119,729	193,029	2,264	31,028	159,738
February	-60,311	-2,206	-19,609	-38,497	130,367	188	11,065	119,114	190,679	2,394	30,673	157,611
March	-62,558	-1,302	-19,025	-42,231	135,608	1,178	11,466	122,964	198,166	2,479	30,491	165,196
April	-65,599	-925	-18,049	-46,625	135,096	1,204	11,785	122,106	200,695	2,129	29,835	168,731
May	-63,107	-869	-15,167	-47,071	136,933	1,266	13,158	122,509	200,040	2,135	28,325	169,580
June	-60,605	-971	-14,674	-44,960	136,685	1,154	12,703	122,828	197,290	2,125	27,377	167,788
July	-59,576	-843	-14,475	-44,259	139,069	1,300	13,837	123,932	198,645	2,143	28,311	168,191
August	-59,795	-1,208	-13,128	-45,459	139,027	819	14,130	124,078	198,822	2,027	27,257	169,538
September	-62,700	-1,394	-14,017	-47,289	136,038	745	12,347	122,946	198,739	2,138	26,365	170,236
October (R)	-61,613	-1,211	-15,203	-45,198	138,580	876	10,982	126,722	200,192	2,087	26,185	171,920
November	-58,279	-1,145	-11,437	-45,697	136,730	942	11,629	124,160	195,009	2,087	23,065	169,857
December												

(1) The petroleum products aggregated in the end-use commodity classification system include virtually the same energy-related petroleum products as those aggregated in the Standard International Trade Classification (SITC). The end-use petroleum products, however, include some products such as ethane, butane, benzene, and toluene, which are included in "Manufactured Goods" in the SITC.

NOTE: For information on data sources, nonsampling errors, definitions and details concerning what is included in the Net Adjustments, see the information section on page A-1 of this release or at www.census.gov/ft900 or www.bea.gov/newsreleases/international/trade/tradnewsrelease.htm.

Exhibit 10. Real Exports and Imports of Goods by Principal End-Use Category
Chained (2009) Dollars

In millions of dollars. Details may not equal totals due to seasonal adjustment and rounding. The values in this exhibit are subject to periodic change, reflecting revisions to the source information for the monthly deflators. (-) Represents zero or less than one-half of measurement shown. (R) - Revised.

Period	Total Census Basis (1)	End-Use Commodity Category						
		Foods, Feeds, & Beverages	Industrial Supplies (2)	Capital Goods	Automotive Vehicles etc.	Consumer Goods	Other Goods	Residual (3)
		Exports						
2013								
Jan. - Dec.	1,398,203	101,077	392,156	533,116	146,533	181,394	50,466	-6,538
Jan. - Nov.	1,280,416	91,474	359,019	488,808	134,529	166,598	46,302	-6,313
January	113,258	8,388	31,100	44,069	11,775	14,841	3,777	-693
February	113,796	8,275	32,121	43,165	11,925	14,428	4,287	-405
March	113,556	7,865	32,212	43,454	11,791	14,236	4,479	-481
April	115,179	7,742	31,955	44,081	12,198	16,025	3,982	-805
May	115,080	7,565	31,880	44,803	12,482	14,970	4,249	-868
June	118,055	7,774	33,121	45,535	12,158	15,811	4,423	-768
July	117,173	7,901	34,000	44,486	12,019	15,150	4,072	-455
August	117,054	7,917	33,282	44,630	12,553	15,072	4,199	-599
September	116,332	8,969	31,845	44,480	12,618	15,089	3,948	-618
October	120,519	9,501	33,871	44,981	12,481	15,764	4,237	-316
November	120,414	9,579	33,630	45,123	12,528	15,212	4,648	-305
December	117,787	9,602	33,137	44,308	12,004	14,796	4,164	-225
2014								
Jan. - Nov.	1,322,258	95,905	365,954	500,142	139,801	177,768	50,399	-7,710
January	117,057	8,965	33,473	44,398	11,686	14,947	3,873	-285
February	115,066	8,844	31,096	43,686	11,676	16,270	4,203	-711
March	118,215	8,849	31,657	45,854	12,356	16,021	4,372	-895
April	118,535	8,510	32,727	45,484	12,161	15,927	4,468	-742
May	119,884	8,525	32,816	45,229	12,893	16,330	4,874	-782
June	120,241	8,527	33,074	45,221	13,024	16,726	4,469	-801
July	121,948	8,102	33,837	45,766	14,590	15,985	4,558	-889
August	122,952	7,931	34,718	46,688	12,977	16,712	4,770	-843
September	120,773	9,029	33,282	45,525	12,869	16,085	4,652	-668
October (R)	124,069	9,254	33,826	47,261	13,020	16,579	4,902	-772
November	123,519	9,370	35,448	45,030	12,549	16,186	5,258	-322
December								
		Imports						
2013								
Jan. - Dec.	1,969,159	93,179	463,653	566,339	293,818	517,091	70,245	-35,166
Jan. - Nov.	1,804,309	85,596	425,821	518,174	268,651	473,277	64,527	-31,737
January	162,719	7,825	39,678	46,610	22,670	42,612	5,629	-2,306
February	162,640	7,861	38,545	46,946	23,256	43,428	5,438	-2,833
March	158,522	7,691	38,135	45,382	23,206	40,608	5,933	-2,432
April	162,383	7,831	38,261	46,337	23,894	42,798	6,104	-2,843
May	167,012	7,960	39,656	46,683	24,773	44,135	6,552	-2,747
June	162,513	7,819	38,065	47,062	24,351	42,432	5,760	-2,977
July	164,530	7,706	38,821	46,705	24,917	43,254	6,005	-2,879
August	164,707	7,747	38,644	47,906	24,978	42,610	5,853	-3,031
September	166,733	7,684	38,959	48,035	25,627	43,798	5,777	-3,147
October	167,018	7,790	39,215	48,035	25,108	43,829	6,086	-3,045
November	165,531	7,682	37,841	48,472	25,871	43,773	5,390	-3,497
December	164,851	7,583	37,833	48,165	25,167	43,814	5,718	-3,430
2014								
Jan. - Nov.	1,869,726	89,600	424,280	552,789	286,481	491,473	65,417	-40,313
January	165,730	7,734	39,232	48,802	24,265	43,259	5,420	-2,983
February	163,381	7,567	38,986	47,618	24,383	42,130	5,479	-2,783
March	168,980	8,098	39,198	48,934	25,054	44,847	6,105	-3,256
April	172,498	8,298	39,787	49,756	25,880	45,758	6,406	-3,387
May	171,996	8,268	38,540	50,687	27,174	45,429	5,795	-3,896
June	169,144	8,583	37,851	50,430	26,170	44,016	5,874	-3,781
July	169,685	8,442	37,537	50,169	27,716	43,496	6,287	-3,962
August	171,172	8,135	38,543	51,926	26,373	44,166	5,939	-3,911
September	171,626	8,239	38,233	51,017	25,881	46,021	6,229	-3,993
October (R)	174,151	8,305	39,167	52,090	27,147	45,401	5,998	-3,957
November	171,363	7,930	37,205	51,360	26,438	46,949	5,884	-4,403
December								

(1) Detailed data are presented on a Census basis. The information needed to convert to a BOP basis is not available.
(2) Includes petroleum and petroleum products
(3) The "residual" represents the difference between total Census basis exports or imports and the sum of the components. For additional information, see www.census.gov/foreign-trade/aip/priceadj.html

NOTE: For information on data sources, nonsampling errors and definitions, see the information section on page A-1 of this release or at www.census.gov/ft900 or www.bea.gov/newsreleases/international/trade/tradnewsrelease.htm.

Part A: Seasonally Adjusted (by Commodity/Service)

Exhibit 11. Real Exports, Imports, and Balance of Goods, Petroleum and Non-Petroleum End-Use Commodity Category Totals Chained (2009) Dollars

In millions of dollars. Details may not equal totals due to seasonal adjustment and rounding. The values in this exhibit are subject to periodic change, reflecting revisions to the source information for the monthly deflators. (-) Represents zero or less than one-half of measurement shown. (R) - Revised.

Period	Balance				Exports				Imports			
	Total Census Basis (1)	Petroleum	Non-petroleum	Residual (2)	Total Census Basis (1)	Petroleum	Non-petroleum	Residual (2)	Total Census Basis (1)	Petroleum	Non-petroleum	Residual (2)
2012												
Jan. - Dec.	-589,053	-158,179	-466,196	35,321	1,359,379	72,777	1,281,782	4,821	1,948,433	230,955	1,747,977	-30,500
Jan. - Nov.	-543,604	-147,420	-427,230	31,046	1,243,692	65,887	1,173,785	4,020	1,787,296	213,307	1,601,015	-27,026
January	-51,142	-14,933	-38,004	1,795	111,142	5,402	105,664	76	162,284	20,335	143,668	-1,719
February	-46,065	-13,139	-35,553	2,627	111,453	5,591	105,689	173	157,518	18,730	141,242	-2,454
March	-50,631	-13,821	-39,594	2,785	114,716	5,928	108,509	279	165,346	19,749	148,103	-2,506
April	-49,832	-14,255	-37,773	2,197	112,740	5,841	106,615	284	162,571	20,096	144,388	-1,913
May	-49,780	-13,063	-39,861	3,144	113,421	5,907	107,211	303	163,201	18,970	147,072	-2,841
June	-46,875	-12,846	-37,091	3,062	115,960	6,621	108,745	594	162,835	19,468	145,836	-2,469
July	-49,395	-12,880	-39,719	3,203	114,233	6,252	107,509	471	163,628	19,133	147,228	-2,732
August	-51,018	-13,814	-39,930	2,726	111,796	5,617	105,947	232	162,814	19,431	145,877	-2,494
September	-47,617	-12,697	-38,196	3,276	115,366	6,342	108,495	529	162,983	19,039	146,691	-2,747
October	-48,648	-13,258	-38,093	2,703	110,220	5,892	103,920	408	158,868	19,150	142,013	-2,295
November	-52,600	-12,714	-43,416	3,530	112,646	6,493	105,480	673	165,246	19,207	148,896	-2,856
December	-45,449	-10,758	-38,966	4,275	115,687	6,890	107,997	801	161,136	17,648	146,962	-3,474
2013												
Jan. - Dec.	-570,956	-132,201	-490,474	51,719	1,398,203	83,155	1,305,945	9,104	1,969,159	215,356	1,796,420	-42,616
Jan. - Nov.	-523,893	-123,007	-447,282	46,396	1,280,416	75,074	1,197,524	7,819	1,804,309	198,081	1,644,805	-38,578
January	-49,461	-13,241	-39,287	3,067	113,258	5,675	107,323	260	162,719	18,916	146,610	-2,807
February	-48,844	-11,829	-40,912	3,896	113,796	6,249	107,002	545	162,640	18,078	147,913	-3,351
March	-44,966	-11,972	-36,479	3,486	113,556	5,745	107,529	282	158,522	17,718	144,008	-3,204
April	-47,204	-11,874	-39,141	3,811	115,179	6,082	108,685	411	162,383	17,956	147,826	-3,399
May	-51,932	-12,370	-43,419	3,858	115,080	6,533	107,934	614	167,012	18,903	151,353	-3,244
June	-44,458	-10,367	-38,554	4,463	118,055	7,253	109,937	866	162,513	17,620	148,491	-3,598
July	-47,357	-10,538	-41,334	4,514	117,173	7,509	108,665	999	164,530	18,046	149,999	-3,516
August	-47,653	-10,358	-41,971	4,676	117,054	7,347	108,785	922	164,707	17,705	150,756	-3,754
September	-50,401	-10,952	-43,989	4,540	116,332	6,983	108,601	748	166,733	17,935	152,590	-3,793
October	-46,499	-10,246	-41,056	4,803	120,519	7,827	111,617	1,074	167,018	18,074	152,673	-3,728
November	-45,117	-9,260	-41,139	5,282	120,414	7,870	111,447	1,098	165,531	17,130	152,585	-4,184
December	-47,063	-9,194	-43,193	5,323	117,787	8,081	108,421	1,285	164,851	17,275	151,614	-4,038
2014												
Jan. - Nov.	-547,468	-103,271	-504,625	60,429	1,322,258	83,579	1,229,052	9,628	1,869,726	186,850	1,733,677	-50,801
January	-48,672	-11,043	-41,960	4,331	117,057	7,114	109,195	748	165,730	18,158	151,156	-3,583
February	-48,315	-11,764	-40,317	3,766	115,066	6,342	108,365	359	163,381	18,107	148,682	-3,407
March	-50,765	-11,379	-43,774	4,388	118,215	6,565	111,252	397	168,980	17,944	155,026	-3,991
April	-53,963	-10,635	-48,406	5,078	118,535	7,251	110,532	752	172,498	17,886	158,938	-4,326
May	-52,112	-8,920	-49,108	5,916	119,884	8,016	110,783	1,086	171,996	16,935	159,890	-4,829
June	-48,903	-8,178	-46,848	6,123	120,241	7,826	111,427	988	169,144	16,005	158,275	-5,136
July	-47,737	-7,820	-46,184	6,267	121,948	8,437	112,270	1,241	169,685	16,257	158,454	-5,026
August	-48,221	-7,706	-46,906	6,392	122,952	8,830	112,718	1,403	171,172	16,536	159,625	-4,989
September	-50,853	-8,559	-48,402	6,108	120,773	7,757	112,051	964	171,626	16,317	160,453	-5,143
October (R)	-50,082	-9,700	-46,095	5,713	124,069	7,166	116,256	647	174,151	16,866	162,351	-5,066
November	-47,844	-7,565	-46,626	6,347	123,519	8,274	114,203	1,042	171,363	15,839	160,829	-5,305
December												

(1) Detailed data are presented on a Census basis. The information needed to convert to a BOP basis is not available.
(2) The "residual" represents the difference between total Census basis exports or imports and the sum of the components. For additional information, see www.census.gov/foreign-trade/aip/priceadj.html.

NOTE: For information on data sources, nonsampling errors and definitions, see the information section on page A-1 of this release or at www.census.gov/ft900 or www.bea.gov/newsreleases/international/trade/tradnewsrelease.htm.

Part B: NOT Seasonally Adjusted

Exhibit 12. U.S. Trade in Goods

In millions of dollars. Details may not equal totals due to rounding. (R) - Revised.

Period	Balance		Exports			Imports		
	Total Balance of Payments Basis	Total Census Basis	Total Balance of Payments Basis	Net Adjustments	Total Census Basis	Total Balance of Payments Basis	Net Adjustments	Total Census Basis
2012								
Jan. - Dec.	-742,095	-730,599	1,561,689	15,986	1,545,703	2,303,785	27,482	2,276,302
Jan. - Nov.	-694,795	-684,213	1,429,765	14,790	1,414,975	2,124,560	25,372	2,099,188
January	-66,787	-65,686	119,206	1,359	117,847	185,993	2,460	183,533
February	-48,935	-48,217	125,053	1,440	123,613	173,988	2,158	171,829
March	-58,235	-57,096	141,511	1,256	140,254	199,745	2,395	197,350
April	-62,764	-62,052	128,975	1,559	127,416	191,739	2,272	189,468
May	-68,319	-67,178	132,372	1,139	131,232	200,691	2,280	198,411
June	-60,183	-59,212	133,895	1,318	132,577	194,078	2,290	191,788
July	-72,135	-71,440	122,963	1,563	121,400	195,098	2,258	192,840
August	-67,304	-66,375	130,015	1,429	128,585	197,319	2,359	194,960
September	-58,418	-57,431	129,585	1,330	128,254	188,003	2,317	185,686
October	-66,345	-65,141	134,823	1,197	133,627	201,168	2,400	198,768
November	-65,370	-64,385	131,368	1,198	130,170	196,738	2,183	194,555
December	-47,301	-46,386	131,924	1,196	130,728	179,225	2,110	177,114
2013								
Jan. - Dec.	-701,669	-688,728	1,592,784	13,191	1,579,593	2,294,453	26,131	2,268,321
Jan. - Nov.	-649,878	-638,219	1,459,755	12,118	1,447,637	2,109,633	23,777	2,085,856
January	-62,670	-62,060	124,580	1,450	123,130	187,250	2,060	185,190
February	-48,176	-46,822	124,407	871	123,536	172,583	2,225	170,358
March	-46,077	-45,093	137,937	1,174	136,762	184,013	2,158	181,855
April	-62,199	-61,096	130,494	1,030	129,465	192,693	2,132	190,561
May	-64,719	-63,679	133,996	989	133,007	198,715	2,029	196,686
June	-51,520	-50,135	135,481	652	134,830	187,001	2,037	184,965
July	-71,010	-70,026	128,569	1,211	127,358	199,578	2,194	197,384
August	-61,475	-60,506	133,942	1,338	132,604	195,417	2,306	193,110
September	-64,456	-63,453	129,653	1,138	128,515	194,109	2,141	191,968
October	-64,234	-62,916	143,121	939	142,182	207,355	2,256	205,098
November	-53,343	-52,432	137,575	1,326	136,249	190,919	2,238	188,681
December	-51,791	-50,509	133,029	1,073	131,956	184,820	2,355	182,465
2014								
Jan. - Nov.	-672,171	-659,379	1,500,906	11,273	1,489,634	2,173,077	24,064	2,149,013
January	-57,873	-57,193	129,057	1,549	127,508	186,930	2,229	184,701
February	-48,104	-45,937	123,861	133	123,728	171,966	2,301	169,665
March	-52,797	-51,441	143,069	1,164	141,905	195,866	2,519	193,346
April	-67,610	-66,700	135,050	1,233	133,817	202,660	2,143	200,517
May	-62,701	-61,852	139,517	1,292	138,225	202,218	2,141	200,077
June	-59,997	-59,046	139,573	1,173	138,400	199,569	2,123	197,446
July	-71,580	-70,762	134,829	1,339	133,491	206,410	2,157	204,253
August	-59,900	-58,657	138,733	855	137,878	198,633	2,097	196,536
September	-70,800	-69,389	134,160	735	133,425	204,960	2,145	202,814
October (R)	-66,176	-64,907	146,716	887	145,829	212,892	2,156	210,736
November	-54,633	-53,493	136,341	913	135,428	190,974	2,053	188,921
December								
October data as published last month:								
	-67,267	-65,933	146,155	825	145,331	213,422	2,158	211,264

NOTE: For information on data sources, nonsampling errors, definitions and details concerning what is included in the Net Adjustments, see the information section on page A-1 of this release or at www.census.gov/ft900 or www.bea.gov/newsreleases/international/trade/tradnewsrelease.htm.

Part B: NOT Seasonally Adjusted

Exhibit 13. Exports and Imports of Goods by Principal End-Use Category

In millions of dollars. Details may not equal totals due to rounding. (R) - Revised.

Period	Total Balance of Payments Basis	Net Adjustments	Total Census Basis (1)	End-Use Commodity Category					
				Foods, Feeds, & Beverages	Industrial Supplies (2)	Capital Goods	Automotive Vehicles, etc.	Consumer Goods	Other Goods
				Exports					
2013									
Jan. - Dec.	1,592,784	13,191	1,579,593	136,184	509,313	534,205	152,556	189,090	58,245
Jan. - Nov.	1,459,755	12,118	1,447,637	122,718	466,801	488,913	140,930	174,856	53,419
January	124,580	1,450	123,130	11,911	40,544	41,242	10,441	14,634	4,358
February	124,407	871	123,536	11,392	41,007	39,630	12,040	14,485	4,982
March	137,937	1,174	136,762	10,862	44,458	46,489	13,553	16,147	5,253
April	130,494	1,030	129,465	9,642	42,352	43,304	13,408	16,173	4,586
May	133,996	989	133,007	9,498	43,084	45,729	13,914	15,905	4,877
June	135,481	652	134,830	9,111	41,945	47,522	13,065	18,091	5,096
July	128,569	1,211	127,358	9,751	43,403	43,869	10,633	15,034	4,668
August	133,942	1,338	132,604	10,022	43,694	45,415	13,343	15,297	4,833
September	129,653	1,138	128,515	10,584	40,590	43,895	13,272	15,625	4,549
October	143,121	939	142,182	14,798	44,308	46,910	13,950	17,328	4,889
November	137,575	1,326	136,249	15,148	41,416	44,908	13,312	16,138	5,327
December	133,029	1,073	131,956	13,465	42,512	45,292	11,626	14,234	4,826
2014									
Jan. - Nov.	1,500,906	11,273	1,489,634	131,021	467,712	502,469	146,841	183,728	57,865
January	129,057	1,549	127,508	13,077	43,390	41,622	10,430	14,583	4,406
February	123,861	133	123,728	12,205	38,777	40,109	11,834	15,985	4,818
March	143,069	1,164	141,905	12,615	43,599	48,966	14,219	17,384	5,121
April	135,050	1,233	133,817	11,406	42,649	45,132	13,382	16,105	5,143
May	139,517	1,292	138,225	11,124	43,576	46,528	14,455	16,900	5,642
June	139,573	1,173	138,400	10,425	42,400	47,270	14,228	18,908	5,169
July	134,829	1,339	133,491	10,279	43,557	45,710	12,914	15,768	5,262
August	138,733	855	137,878	10,242	44,563	47,258	13,745	16,570	5,499
September	134,160	735	133,425	10,492	41,369	45,638	13,764	16,841	5,321
October (R)	146,716	887	145,829	14,524	43,363	49,619	14,559	18,176	5,589
November	136,341	913	135,428	14,632	40,469	44,617	13,310	16,507	5,894
December									
				Imports					
2013									
Jan. - Dec.	2,294,453	26,131	2,268,321	115,146	681,576	554,518	308,802	532,743	75,537
Jan. - Nov.	2,109,633	23,777	2,085,856	105,360	629,545	507,052	283,388	490,894	69,618
January	187,250	2,060	185,190	9,525	60,468	43,701	22,114	43,297	6,086
February	172,583	2,225	170,358	8,849	51,923	40,812	23,482	39,869	5,422
March	184,013	2,158	181,855	9,838	56,834	44,985	25,917	37,547	6,734
April	192,693	2,132	190,561	9,840	59,398	45,757	25,954	42,811	6,801
May	198,715	2,029	196,686	10,347	60,743	46,637	25,973	45,803	7,183
June	187,001	2,037	184,965	9,418	55,680	46,602	25,516	41,545	6,205
July	199,578	2,194	197,384	9,607	60,470	47,971	24,962	47,912	6,463
August	195,417	2,306	193,110	9,358	58,443	46,836	26,956	45,494	6,023
September	194,109	2,141	191,968	8,966	56,186	46,530	26,174	47,837	6,276
October	207,355	2,256	205,098	10,107	58,387	49,245	28,183	52,324	6,853
November	190,919	2,238	188,681	9,505	51,013	47,975	28,158	46,456	5,573
December	184,820	2,355	182,465	9,786	52,031	47,466	25,414	41,849	5,918
2014									
Jan. - Nov.	2,173,077	24,064	2,149,013	114,782	613,813	539,048	299,755	510,821	70,796
January	186,930	2,229	184,701	9,956	56,767	45,111	23,236	43,814	5,817
February	171,966	2,301	169,665	8,826	51,045	41,191	24,288	38,889	5,426
March	195,866	2,519	193,346	10,967	57,798	48,394	27,782	41,447	6,959
April	202,660	2,143	200,517	10,952	60,417	48,629	27,799	45,567	7,152
May	202,218	2,141	200,077	10,968	58,433	49,935	28,121	46,377	6,242
June	199,569	2,123	197,446	10,874	56,485	51,201	27,817	44,575	6,494
July	206,410	2,157	204,253	10,762	59,737	51,248	27,376	48,259	6,872
August	198,633	2,097	196,536	10,076	56,223	49,776	27,950	46,491	6,020
September	204,960	2,145	202,814	10,135	55,257	50,900	27,000	52,497	7,025
October (R)	212,892	2,156	210,736	11,170	55,228	53,167	30,273	54,064	6,834
November	190,974	2,053	188,921	10,096	46,422	49,496	28,113	48,841	5,955
December									

(1) Detailed data are presented on a Census basis. The information needed to convert to a BOP basis is not available.
(2) Includes petroleum and petroleum products.

NOTE: For information on data sources, nonsampling errors and definitions, see the information section on page A-1 of this release or at www.census.gov/ft900 or www.bea.gov/newsreleases/international/trade/tradnewsrelease.htm.

Part B: NOT Seasonally Adjusted

Exhibit 14. Exports, Imports, and Balance of Goods by Selected Countries and Areas: 2014

In millions of dollars. Details may not equal totals due to rounding. (-) Represents zero or less than one-half of measurement shown.
(R) - Revised. (X) - Not applicable.

Item (1)	Balance					Exports					Imports		
	November 2014		October 2014	Year-to-Date 2014		November 2014		October 2014	Year-to-Date 2014		November 2014		October 2014	Year-to-Date 2014
Total Balance of Payments Basis	-54,633	(R)	-66,176	-672,171		136,341	(R)	146,716	1,500,906		190,974	(R)	212,892	2,173,077
Net Adjustments	-1,140	(R)	-1,269	-12,791		913	(R)	887	11,273		2,053	(R)	2,156	24,064
Total Census Basis	-53,493	(R)	-64,907	-659,379		135,428	(R)	145,829	1,489,634		188,921	(R)	210,736	2,149,013
North America	-5,646	(R)	-7,411	-78,448		45,303	(R)	50,613	509,256		50,949		58,024	587,704
Canada	-1,197	(R)	-2,257	-29,589		25,580	(R)	28,356	287,819		26,778		30,613	317,408
Mexico	-4,449		-5,155	-48,859		19,722		22,257	221,437		24,171		27,411	270,296
Europe	-11,806		-15,042	-141,302		27,254		28,250	307,989		39,060		43,291	449,291
European Union	-11,803		-12,740	-127,503		22,128		23,968	254,552		33,931		36,708	382,054
Austria	-694		-646	-6,408		213		270	3,538		906		917	9,946
Belgium	1,338		1,241	13,030		2,917		3,178	32,249		1,579		1,937	19,219
Czech Republic	-163		-204	-1,794		170		190	2,140		333		394	3,933
Finland	-197		-262	-2,575		165		149	1,976		362		412	4,551
France	-1,509		-1,379	-14,367		2,326		2,830	28,686		3,835		4,209	43,053
Germany	-6,519		-6,928	-67,390		3,996		3,988	45,668		10,515		10,916	113,058
Hungary	-297		-353	-3,104		142		162	1,679		440		515	4,782
Ireland	-1,891		-1,806	-23,175		550		807	7,227		2,440		2,612	30,402
Italy	-2,387		-2,326	-22,890		1,280		1,421	15,574		3,667		3,747	38,464
Netherlands	2,291		1,539	20,866		3,811		3,472	40,031		1,520		1,933	19,165
Poland	-126		-145	-1,354		298		308	3,362		425		452	4,715
Spain	-411		-158	-3,781		889		980	9,341		1,300		1,138	13,123
Sweden	-393		-607	-5,320		351		366	4,001		744		973	9,321
United Kingdom	-84		-15	52		4,220		4,799	49,250		4,305		4,814	49,197
Other	-761		-691	-9,293		800		1,048	9,832		1,561		1,739	19,125
Norway	4		-80	-851		353		308	4,139		350		388	4,989
Russia	-203		-896	-11,747		917		1,046	10,220		1,119		1,941	21,967
Switzerland	-4		-1,091	-7,666		2,468		1,743	20,815		2,471		2,834	28,481
Other Europe	200		-235	6,464		1,389		1,185	18,263		1,189		1,420	11,800
Euro Area	-10,301		-10,803	-109,407		16,552		17,758	189,807		26,853		28,561	299,213
Pacific Rim Countries	-36,140		-39,158	-377,404		33,816		36,852	360,776		69,955		76,010	738,180
Australia	1,241		1,387	14,987		2,133		2,404	24,680		892		1,017	9,692
China	-29,937		-32,554	-314,332		12,190		12,690	111,793		42,127		45,244	426,125
Indonesia	-831		-1,118	-10,058		670		725	7,800		1,501		1,843	17,858
Japan	-5,522		-6,447	-61,273		5,072		5,619	61,186		10,593		12,066	122,459
Malaysia	-1,665		-1,656	-15,648		1,106		1,224	11,914		2,771		2,880	27,562
Philippines	-133		-146	-1,493		689		741	7,770		822		887	9,263
Newly Industrialized Countries (NICs)	661		1,250	9,376		11,618		13,015	130,826		10,957		11,765	121,449
Hong Kong	2,974		3,397	32,188		3,328		3,959	37,579		354		561	5,391
Korea, South	-2,804		-2,515	-22,838		3,504		3,559	40,721		6,309		6,075	63,559
Singapore	1,501		1,510	12,919		2,595		2,957	28,067		1,094		1,447	15,148
Taiwan	-1,009		-1,142	-12,892		2,190		2,540	24,459		3,200		3,682	37,351
Other	47		126	1,037		339		434	4,808		293		308	3,771
South/Central America	4,924		3,092	31,467		15,305		15,980	169,782		10,380		12,888	138,314
Argentina	550		326	6,072		862		783	9,983		312		457	3,911
Brazil	746		1,108	11,756		3,197		3,880	39,281		2,451		2,772	27,525
Chile	1,027		372	6,644		1,577		1,109	15,360		549		737	8,716
Colombia	255		236	1,781		1,632		1,759	18,394		1,377		1,523	16,613
Other	2,345		1,050	5,214		8,037		8,449	86,764		5,691		7,400	81,550
OPEC	-781		-1,761	-48,034		6,908		7,816	74,946		7,689		9,577	122,981
Nigeria	342		393	2,079		468		570	5,539		126		177	3,460
Saudi Arabia	-1,145		-1,076	-27,637		1,489		1,606	16,424		2,634		2,683	44,061
Venezuela	-577		-1,346	-18,049		1,088		1,270	10,188		1,665		2,616	28,237
Other	598		269	-4,428		3,863		4,371	42,795		3,265		4,102	47,223
Africa	765		528	3,550		3,223		3,353	35,148		2,458		2,825	31,599
Algeria	(-)		-193	-1,811		262		200	2,418		263		394	4,229
Egypt	349		558	4,737		442		668	6,033		93		111	1,296
South Africa	-189		-48	-1,618		544		568	5,858		733		616	7,476
Other	605		212	2,242		1,975		1,916	20,840		1,369		1,705	18,598
Other Countries	-5,461		-7,660	-72,565		6,249		5,764	60,033		11,710		13,423	132,598
India	-1,122		-2,199	-22,098		2,224		2,031	19,664		3,346		4,230	41,762
Thailand	-1,218		-1,428	-14,038		966		1,045	10,601		2,184		2,472	24,639
Other	-3,121		-4,033	-36,428		3,059		2,688	29,768		6,180		6,721	66,197
Unidentified Countries (2)	(-)		(-)	(-)		(-)		(-)	(-)		(X)		(X)	(X)
Timing Adjustments	(X)		632	250		(X)		104	-32		(X)		-528	-282

(1) Detailed data are presented on a Census basis. The information needed to convert to a BOP basis is not available.
(2) The export totals reflect shipments of certain grains, oilseeds, and satellites that are not included in the country/area totals.

NOTES:
* This exhibit is not additive; countries may be included in more than one area. For a list of countries in each area, see the information section on page A-2 of this release or at www.census.gov/ft900 or www.bea.gov/newsreleases/international/trade/tradnewsrelease.htm.
* Area data reflect the composition of the areas as they were at the time of reporting.
* For information on data sources, nonsampling errors and definitions, see the information section on page A-1 of this release or at www.census.gov/ft900 or www.bea.gov/newsreleases/international/trade/tradnewsrelease.htm.

Part B: NOT Seasonally Adjusted

Exhibit 14a. Exports, Imports, and Balance of Goods by Selected Countries and Areas: 2013

In millions of dollars. Details may not equal totals due to rounding. (-) Represents zero or less than one-half of measurement shown.
(X) - Not applicable.

Item (1)	Balance			Exports			Imports		
	November 2013	October 2013	Year-to-Date 2013	November 2013	October 2013	Year-to-Date 2013	November 2013	October 2013	Year-to-Date 2013
Total Balance of Payments Basis	**-53,343**	**-64,234**	**-649,878**	**137,575**	**143,121**	**1,459,755**	**190,919**	**207,355**	**2,109,633**
Net Adjustments	-911	-1,318	-11,659	1,326	939	12,118	2,238	2,256	23,777
Total Census Basis	**-52,432**	**-62,916**	**-638,219**	**136,249**	**142,182**	**1,447,637**	**188,681**	**205,098**	**2,085,856**
North America	-6,082	-6,717	-78,105	45,027	48,211	485,879	51,109	54,928	563,985
Canada	-1,662	-2,503	-27,691	25,724	27,118	277,893	27,387	29,622	305,584
Mexico	-4,419	-4,214	-50,415	19,303	21,093	207,986	23,722	25,307	258,401
Europe	-10,344	-15,204	-122,467	28,136	28,543	301,154	38,479	43,746	423,620
European Union	-10,325	-13,755	-114,160	22,744	23,303	241,351	33,069	37,058	355,511
Austria	-667	-678	-5,673	208	199	3,331	875	878	9,004
Belgium	1,089	880	11,876	2,682	2,723	29,368	1,594	1,843	17,492
Czech Republic	-119	-200	-1,791	218	176	1,792	337	375	3,583
Finland	-229	-200	-2,152	184	198	2,192	413	397	4,344
France	-1,015	-1,641	-12,433	2,781	2,935	28,981	3,796	4,576	41,414
Germany	-5,990	-6,839	-61,194	4,394	4,045	43,730	10,384	10,884	104,924
Hungary	-253	-244	-1,791	127	153	1,583	380	397	3,374
Ireland	-1,835	-2,797	-23,155	555	611	6,031	2,391	3,408	29,186
Italy	-1,984	-2,303	-19,939	1,336	1,278	15,391	3,320	3,581	35,330
Netherlands	2,263	2,478	21,263	3,852	4,232	39,137	1,589	1,754	17,874
Poland	-40	-190	-940	349	283	3,532	389	473	4,472
Spain	49	-82	-1,446	933	950	9,231	884	1,032	10,677
Sweden	-554	-485	-4,424	291	367	3,994	844	852	8,418
United Kingdom	-372	-721	-4,502	3,904	4,262	43,967	4,277	4,983	48,469
Other	-668	-734	-7,859	929	890	9,090	1,597	1,624	16,949
Norway	-90	-339	-980	398	347	4,163	488	686	5,143
Russia	-904	-1,588	-15,463	950	1,047	10,145	1,854	2,635	25,608
Switzerland	-132	-261	-727	2,085	2,190	25,275	2,217	2,451	26,002
Other Europe	1,108	739	8,863	1,958	1,656	20,219	850	917	11,357
Euro Area	-8,524	-11,376	-95,114	17,339	17,611	181,953	25,863	28,987	277,067
Pacific Rim Countries	-31,133	-34,087	-355,263	36,015	36,514	352,281	67,148	70,601	707,544
Australia	1,182	1,479	15,221	2,008	2,246	23,751	825	767	8,530
China	-27,043	-28,743	-294,220	13,065	13,105	108,730	40,107	41,849	402,950
Indonesia	-772	-848	-9,063	701	1,068	8,353	1,473	1,917	17,416
Japan	-5,763	-6,412	-67,463	5,844	5,501	59,946	11,607	11,912	127,409
Malaysia	-1,142	-1,288	-12,939	1,044	1,173	11,996	2,187	2,461	24,935
Philippines	149	-197	-833	913	666	7,691	764	863	8,525
Newly Industrialized Countries (NICs)	2,005	1,682	13,485	11,891	12,230	127,848	9,886	10,548	114,363
Hong Kong	2,850	3,096	33,342	3,229	3,494	38,669	379	399	5,327
Korea, South	-1,174	-1,672	-19,775	3,884	3,520	37,742	5,058	5,192	57,517
Singapore	1,154	1,311	11,653	2,495	2,874	28,261	1,342	1,563	16,608
Taiwan	-826	-1,053	-11,734	2,283	2,342	23,176	3,109	3,395	34,911
Other	250	240	549	549	524	3,965	298	284	3,416
South/Central America	2,826	2,635	22,049	14,810	15,679	168,282	11,985	13,044	146,234
Argentina	348	476	5,061	808	853	9,345	460	378	4,284
Brazil	1,045	1,669	15,003	3,123	3,943	40,413	2,078	2,273	25,410
Chile	831	981	6,614	1,385	1,567	16,208	554	587	9,594
Colombia	178	-154	-3,590	1,632	1,609	16,599	1,454	1,763	20,188
Other	424	-336	-1,039	7,862	7,707	85,718	7,438	8,044	86,757
OPEC	-4,816	-5,563	-64,022	6,486	7,242	77,258	11,303	12,805	141,279
Nigeria	195	-152	-5,642	663	603	5,846	468	754	11,488
Saudi Arabia	-2,856	-3,095	-30,062	1,500	1,625	16,972	4,356	4,720	47,034
Venezuela	-1,547	-1,913	-17,223	1,072	1,051	12,208	2,619	2,964	29,431
Other	-609	-403	-11,095	3,252	3,963	42,231	3,860	4,366	53,326
Africa	25	-524	-15,117	2,764	3,124	32,285	2,739	3,648	47,403
Algeria	-326	-210	-2,747	89	142	1,737	414	353	4,483
Egypt	286	289	3,243	382	417	4,753	96	127	1,510
South Africa	-32	-50	-984	452	596	6,810	484	646	7,794
Other	97	-553	-14,629	1,841	1,969	18,986	1,744	2,522	33,615
Other Countries	-5,253	-6,734	-63,639	5,515	5,344	59,090	10,768	12,078	122,729
India	-1,007	-1,949	-18,547	1,855	1,742	20,283	2,863	3,690	38,830
Thailand	-1,319	-1,336	-13,099	960	1,063	10,902	2,279	2,400	24,001
Other	-2,926	-3,449	-31,993	2,700	2,539	27,905	5,626	5,988	59,898
Unidentified Countries (2)	61	73	141	61	73	141	(X)	(X)	(X)

(1) Detailed data are presented on a Census basis. The information needed to convert to a BOP basis is not available.
(2) The export totals reflect shipments of certain grains, oilseeds, and satellites that are not included in the country/area totals.

NOTES:

* This exhibit is not additive; countries may be included in more than one area. For a list of countries in each area, see the information section on page A-2 of this release or at www.census.gov/ft900 or www.bea.gov/newsreleases/international/trade/tradnewsrelease.htm.
* Area data reflect the composition of the areas at yearend.
* For information on data sources, nonsampling errors and definitions, see the information section on page A-1 of this release or at www.census.gov/ft900 or www.bea.gov/newsreleases/international/trade/tradnewsrelease.htm.

Part B: NOT Seasonally Adjusted

Exhibit 15. Exports and Imports of Goods by Principal Commodities

In millions of dollars. Details may not equal totals due to rounding. This exhibit is not additive.
(R) - Revised. (X) - Not applicable. (-) Represents zero or less than one-half of measurement shown.

Item (1)	2014						2013	
	November		October		Year-to-Date		Year-to-Date	
	Exports	Imports	Exports	Imports	Exports	Imports	Exports	Imports
Total Balance of Payment Basis (2)	136,341	190,974 (R)	146,716 (R)	212,892	1,500,906	2,173,077	1,459,755	2,109,633
Net Adjustments (2)	913	2,053 (R)	887 (R)	2,156	11,273	24,064	12,118	23,777
Total Census Basis (2)	135,428	188,921 (R)	145,829 (R)	210,736	1,489,634	2,149,013	1,447,637	2,085,856
Manufactured Goods (3)	97,415	159,889	105,369	176,587	1,095,796	1,763,884	1,086,332	1,682,752
Agricultural Commodities (3)	14,887	8,828	14,453	9,654	136,533	102,302	130,059	95,988
Food and Live Animals	8,631	7,855	9,443	8,542	99,996	88,358	94,401	80,572
Live animals other than fish	69	418	117	363	793	3,128	852	2,344
Meat and preparations	1,599	837	1,764	878	17,720	7,981	16,419	6,003
Dairy products and birds' eggs	441	187	455	205	5,879	1,771	5,361	1,611
Fish and preparations	431	1,662	579	1,907	5,041	18,373	4,913	16,067
Cereals and preparations	1,697	738	1,866	824	25,023	8,462	22,200	8,975
Vegetables and fruit	2,260	2,188	2,372	2,221	20,283	25,615	19,775	24,107
Sugars, preparations and honey	169	297	201	402	2,060	4,193	2,247	4,016
Coffee, tea, cocoa and spices	279	939	319	1,091	2,881	11,948	2,844	10,798
Feeding stuff for animals	961	218	988	255	12,157	2,858	11,928	2,637
Miscellaneous edible products	725	369	782	396	8,159	4,028	7,860	4,015
Beverages and Tobacco	530	1,808	580	2,137	5,922	19,885	5,948	19,169
Beverages	388	1,600	469	1,903	4,589	17,976	4,475	17,142
Tobacco and manufactures	141	207	111	234	1,333	1,909	1,473	2,027
Crude Materials Except Fuels	9,761	2,705	9,170	3,052	77,464	33,690	76,409	32,266
Hides, skins and furskins, raw	192	14	211	11	2,714	289	2,923	272
Oil seeds and oleaginous fruits	5,142	105	4,100	99	22,576	2,075	20,107	1,534
Crude rubber	237	262	270	280	2,915	3,514	3,002	3,937
Cork and wood	560	558	640	664	6,747	6,598	6,006	5,889
Pulp and waste paper	742	248	766	280	8,006	3,286	7,939	3,335
Textile fibers, including waste	421	116	358	121	6,341	1,299	7,607	1,200
Crude fertilizers	226	260	275	285	2,576	2,709	2,267	2,402
Metalliferous ores and metal scrap	1,961	632	2,260	802	22,710	8,193	23,824	7,683
Crude animal and vegetable materials	280	510	290	511	2,878	5,728	2,734	6,014
Mineral Fuels and Lubricants	11,878	22,156	12,066	27,165	143,573	320,670	132,109	350,684
Coal, coke and briquettes	642	113	722	84	8,157	1,121	10,597	938
Petroleum products and preparations	10,160	20,743	9,889	25,888	118,477	302,950	109,902	335,957
Gas, natural and manufactured	1,056	1,143	1,430	1,025	16,377	14,148	11,306	11,582
Electric current	21	157	24	167	563	2,451	303	2,206
Animal and Vegetables Oils	231	405	215	566	2,586	5,346	2,875	5,258
Animal oils and fats	53	16	57	20	676	226	703	246
Fixed vegetable fats and oils, crude	153	374	126	533	1,553	4,980	1,773	4,870
Animal or vegetables fats, processed	25	15	32	14	358	139	399	143
Chemicals and Related Products	16,124	15,545	17,997	18,006	186,996	190,005	183,484	180,709
Organic chemicals	3,083	3,431	3,573	4,222	36,340	48,258	38,934	48,683
Inorganic chemicals	942	1,002	1,012	1,163	10,311	11,814	10,299	13,253
Dyeing, tanning and coloring materials	608	293	670	336	7,119	3,686	7,012	3,513
Medicinial and pharmaceutical products	3,851	5,916	4,304	6,660	42,784	69,065	38,573	61,443
Essential oils and resinoids	1,258	1,067	1,379	1,209	14,167	12,214	13,693	11,447
Fertilizers	276	619	321	803	3,431	7,422	3,745	7,504
Plastics in primary forms	2,722	1,198	2,957	1,420	32,405	14,500	31,868	12,966
Plastics in nonprimary forms	1,026	742	1,140	847	11,838	8,884	11,185	8,246
Chemical materials and products	2,359	1,277	2,641	1,347	28,602	14,162	28,175	13,654

Part B: NOT Seasonally Adjusted

Exhibit 15. Exports and Imports of Goods by Principal Commodities

In millions of dollars. Details may not equal totals due to rounding. This exhibit is not additive.
(R) - Revised. (X) - Not applicable. (-) Represents zero or less than one-half of measurement shown.

Item (1)	2014						2013	
	November		October		Year-to-Date		Year-to-Date	
	Exports	Imports	Exports	Imports	Exports	Imports	Exports	Imports
Manufactured Goods by Material	**9,320**	**20,194**	**10,404**	**23,176**	**108,681**	**233,358**	**107,375**	**216,737**
Leather and leather manufactures	118	116	144	132	1,318	1,286	1,238	1,160
Rubber manufactures (4)	804	1,724	932	1,915	9,442	20,165	9,252	19,414
Cork and wood manufactures	172	756	210	830	2,046	8,786	2,027	8,382
Paper and paperboard	1,226	1,349	1,419	1,562	14,795	15,414	14,946	14,755
Textile yarn, fabrics	1,081	2,174	1,170	2,489	12,312	24,786	11,963	23,760
Nonmetallic mineral manufactures (4)	1,093	3,553	1,137	4,152	12,028	41,560	11,631	38,645
Iron and steel	1,447	3,831	1,583	4,418	16,944	42,857	17,133	33,868
Nonferrous metals	1,200	3,019	1,372	3,422	14,324	35,148	14,527	35,515
Manufactures of metals	2,179	3,672	2,437	4,257	25,472	43,357	24,658	41,238
Machinery and Transport Equipment	**43,411**	**83,132**	**48,049**	**86,727**	**487,872**	**856,525**	**471,493**	**811,867**
Power generating machinery (4)	3,308	5,147	3,754	5,972	36,336	60,779	35,170	55,719
Specialized industrial machinery	3,788	3,702	4,399	3,992	44,798	43,149	44,899	38,591
Metalworking machinery	474	799	506	940	5,217	9,025	5,576	9,073
General industrial machinery	5,603	7,061	6,080	7,965	64,664	84,884	61,407	76,871
Office machines	1,739	11,418	1,925	11,361	19,888	106,939	19,559	106,864
Telecommunications equipment (4)	1,985	16,651	2,110	14,842	21,555	138,026	21,656	134,078
Electrical machinery (4)	6,645	12,986	7,270	14,749	74,182	145,457	72,329	137,743
Road vehicles	9,996	22,407	10,871	23,736	111,591	234,592	109,645	224,046
Transport equipment (4)	9,874	2,961	11,134	3,169	109,640	33,674	101,251	28,882
Miscellaneous Manufactured Articles	**10,206**	**28,529**	**11,276**	**34,029**	**112,565**	**320,743**	**112,124**	**306,704**
Prefabricated buildings	274	937	321	1,102	2,983	10,549	2,896	9,514
Furniture (4)	553	3,365	603	3,599	5,930	37,912	5,654	34,781
Travel goods	55	881	54	1,071	519	10,080	535	9,715
Apparel and clothing accessories	294	6,455	320	8,839	3,143	83,551	3,182	81,524
Footwear	73	1,772	83	2,347	758	24,032	731	22,930
Scientific and controlling equipment (4)	4,079	4,156	4,330	4,514	45,757	46,018	45,923	43,365
Photographic equipment	519	1,292	561	1,365	5,940	13,092	6,053	12,380
Miscellaneous manufactured articles	4,360	9,673	5,003	11,191	47,534	95,508	47,151	92,495
Miscellaneous Commodities	**6,797**	**6,593**	**5,930**	**7,863**	**61,067**	**80,715**	**70,229**	**81,890**
Special transactions	775	4,729	664	5,492	7,238	55,234	6,617	52,398
Coin, including gold coin	47	137	24	164	280	1,532	382	2,306
Coin, other than gold	3	0	3	1	31	13	46	34
Gold, nonmonetary	2,870	900	2,132	1,192	19,973	13,141	31,695	14,762
Low value estimate	3,102	827	3,106	1,014	33,545	10,795	31,489	12,391
Re-Exports	**18,538**	**(X)**	**20,201**	**(X)**	**202,845**	**(X)**	**191,190**	**(X)**
Manufactured Goods (3)	17,464	(X)	19,285	(X)	192,505	(X)	183,120	(X)
Agricultural Commodities (3)	376	(X)	369	(X)	4,166	(X)	3,944	(X)

(1) Detailed data are presented for domestic exports unless otherwise noted. All data are on a Census basis. The information needed to convert to a BOP basis is not available.
(2) Total exports including re-exports (exports of foreign merchandise).
(3) Manufactured Goods is based on the North American Industry Classification System (NAICS) and Agricultural Commodities is based on the Harmonized System commodities specified by the U.S. Department of Agriculture definition. All other commodity detail is based on the SITC.
(4) Due to non-disclosure requirements, certain 10-digit Schedule B commodity classifications are subject to suppression and require a change in aggregation. For additional information, see www.census.gov/foreign-trade/statistics/notices/aircraft.

NOTE: For information on data sources, nonsampling errors and definitions, see the information section on page A-1 of this release or at www.census.gov/ft900 or www.bea.gov/newsreleases/international/trade/tradnewsrelease.htm.

Part B: NOT Seasonally Adjusted

Exhibit 16. Exports, Imports, and Balance of Advanced Technology Products
In millions of dollars. Details may not equal totals due to rounding.

Period	Balance	Exports	Imports
2012			
Jan.- Dec.	-91,218	305,010	396,228
Jan.- Nov.	-85,956	277,471	363,427
January	-6,796	22,563	29,359
February	-5,796	23,433	29,229
March	-7,023	28,060	35,083
April	-6,716	23,768	30,483
May	-8,837	24,887	33,724
June	-6,847	26,554	33,401
July	-8,434	24,583	33,017
August	-6,721	25,600	32,321
September	-7,116	25,815	32,932
October	-9,950	26,109	36,059
November	-11,721	26,099	37,819
December	-5,261	27,539	32,801
2013			
Jan.- Dec.	-81,287	319,789	401,076
Jan.- Nov.	-75,391	291,547	366,938
January	-7,272	24,010	31,282
February	-5,243	22,660	27,903
March	-3,602	27,982	31,585
April	-7,831	24,691	32,521
May	-6,985	27,141	34,127
June	-3,729	29,198	32,926
July	-7,699	26,735	34,434
August	-5,773	26,734	32,507
September	-8,306	26,751	35,057
October	-9,620	27,696	37,316
November	-9,332	27,949	37,282
December	-5,896	28,242	34,138
2014			
Jan.- Nov.	-77,644	304,793	382,437
January	-4,693	25,311	30,004
February	-3,238	24,338	27,576
March	-3,877	29,304	33,181
April	-8,365	26,982	35,348
May	-7,585	27,616	35,200
June	-7,451	28,395	35,845
July	-6,928	27,116	34,045
August	-4,522	28,857	33,378
September	-10,464	28,295	38,760
October	-9,153	30,375	39,528
November	-11,367	28,204	39,571
December			

NOTES:

* Due to non-disclosure requirements, certain 10-digit Schedule B commodity classifications are subject to suppression and require a change in aggregation. As a result, Advanced Technology Product exports are overstated by $369 million in November 2014. For additional information, see www.census.gov/ft900

* Data are not available on a BOP basis. For information on data sources, nonsampling errors and definitions, see the information section on page A-1 of this release or at www.census.gov/ft900 or www.bea.gov/newsreleases/international/trade/tradnewsrelease.htm.

Part B: NOT Seasonally Adjusted

Exhibit 16a. Exports, Imports, and Balance of Advanced Technology Products by Technology Group and Selected Countries and Areas

In millions of dollars. Details may not equal totals due to rounding.

Technology Group	2014									2013		
	November			October			Year-to-Date			Year-to-Date		
	Balance	Exports	Imports	Balance	Exports	Imports	Balance	Exports	Imports	Balance	Exports	Imports
Total	-11,367	28,204	39,571	-9,153	30,375	39,528	-77,644	304,793	382,437	-75,391	291,547	366,938
Advanced Materials	-11	172	183	-21	183	204	-10	1,988	1,998	-75	1,928	2,003
Aerospace (1)	6,440	10,575	4,135	7,142	11,603	4,461	67,032	113,544	46,512	64,567	104,889	40,322
Biotechnology	352	1,245	893	-42	1,330	1,372	1,019	13,340	12,321	169	10,506	10,337
Electronics	494	3,398	2,904	316	3,745	3,429	5,631	39,262	33,632	5,369	38,448	33,079
Flexible Manufacturing	130	1,241	1,111	308	1,494	1,187	687	13,921	13,234	1,854	12,950	11,096
Information and Communications (1)	-16,060	8,057	24,118	-13,462	8,597	22,058	-121,234	86,488	207,722	-120,614	83,824	204,439
Life Science	-844	2,610	3,454	-1,123	2,609	3,732	-12,629	28,241	40,870	-11,018	29,443	40,462
Nuclear Technology	-114	64	178	-161	128	289	-1,571	895	2,465	-1,633	1,610	3,243
Opto-Electronics (1)	-2,164	377	2,540	-2,285	410	2,694	-18,370	4,485	22,856	-16,469	4,630	21,099
Weapons	408	464	56	174	276	103	1,802	2,629	827	2,460	3,318	858

Selected Countries and Areas	2014									2013		
	November			October			Year-to-Date			Year-to-Date		
	Balance	Exports	Imports	Balance	Exports	Imports	Balance	Exports	Imports	Balance	Exports	Imports
Total	-11,367	28,204	39,571	-9,153	30,375	39,528	-77,644	304,793	382,437	-75,391	291,547	366,938
North America	356	5,594	5,238	297	6,397	6,100	5,236	61,007	55,772	2,733	59,807	57,074
Canada	1,585	2,724	1,139	1,425	2,937	1,512	13,427	27,731	14,304	14,348	27,010	12,661
Mexico	-1,230	2,870	4,100	-1,128	3,460	4,588	-8,191	33,276	41,467	-11,616	32,797	44,413
European Union	-85	5,843	5,928	-216	6,707	6,923	-4,718	68,275	72,993	-4,739	63,752	68,491
France	-195	831	1,026	15	1,152	1,136	-1,717	10,182	11,899	-1,052	10,535	11,587
Germany	-410	1,113	1,523	-485	1,010	1,495	-2,845	13,051	15,896	-1,616	11,879	13,495
Ireland	-902	183	1,085	-977	323	1,300	-13,645	2,655	16,300	-16,024	1,480	17,503
Italy	-75	240	315	-45	262	306	-100	3,391	3,491	-76	3,765	3,841
United Kingdom	615	1,214	599	589	1,435	846	5,492	13,827	8,335	4,627	12,691	8,064
Other	882	2,262	1,380	686	2,525	1,839	8,097	25,168	17,071	9,401	23,402	14,001
Pacific Rim Countries	-15,534	9,352	24,886	-13,061	9,939	23,000	-116,149	102,011	218,160	-110,476	97,801	208,276
Australia	408	516	107	363	466	103	3,762	4,937	1,175	3,245	4,370	1,125
China	-14,647	2,492	17,139	-12,612	2,641	15,253	-111,833	27,458	139,291	-106,365	25,893	132,258
Indonesia	55	137	82	206	282	77	1,353	2,139	785	1,398	2,153	755
Japan	-389	1,402	1,790	-699	1,415	2,114	-5,780	15,651	21,431	-4,981	16,520	21,501
Malaysia	-1,188	654	1,842	-1,090	724	1,813	-9,971	6,749	16,720	-7,908	6,667	14,575
Philippines	-73	231	304	-35	284	319	-515	2,799	3,314	101	3,173	3,072
Newly Industrialized Countries (NICs)	217	3,822	3,604	689	3,995	3,306	4,962	40,234	35,272	2,894	37,718	34,825
Hong Kong	994	1,053	58	1,132	1,182	50	10,324	10,761	437	9,429	9,890	460
Korea, South	-758	1,059	1,817	-448	840	1,289	-4,878	10,599	15,477	-4,488	10,426	14,914
Singapore	415	894	480	359	870	511	3,959	9,218	5,259	2,584	8,709	6,125
Taiwan	-433	816	1,249	-354	1,102	1,456	-4,443	9,657	14,099	-4,632	8,694	13,326
Other	82	99	17	117	133	16	1,873	2,044	172	1,140	1,306	166
South/Central America	1,941	2,545	604	1,580	2,292	712	17,153	25,966	8,814	17,545	27,392	9,846
Brazil	544	837	294	712	926	214	7,571	9,558	1,987	9,249	10,640	1,391
Other	1,398	1,707	310	868	1,366	498	9,581	16,408	6,827	8,297	16,752	8,455
Other Countries	1,956	4,871	2,915	2,247	5,041	2,794	20,835	47,534	26,699	19,546	42,796	23,250
India	513	651	138	225	354	129	2,667	4,322	1,655	2,997	4,501	1,503
Israel	-71	244	315	-33	265	298	-69	3,120	3,189	-29	2,764	2,792
Thailand	-639	224	863	-593	401	994	-5,557	3,844	9,401	-5,567	3,593	9,160
Other	2,152	3,751	1,599	2,647	4,020	1,373	23,794	36,248	12,454	22,144	31,938	9,795

(1) Due to non-disclosure requirements, certain 10-digit Schedule B commodity classifications are subject to suppression and require a change in aggregation. As a result, Advanced Technology Product exports are overstated by $369 million in November 2014. For additional information, see www.census.gov/ft900.

NOTE: Data are not available on a BOP basis. For information on data sources, nonsampling errors and definitions, see the information section on page A-1 of this release or at www.census.gov/ft900 or www.bea.gov/newsreleases/international/trade/tradnewsrelease.htm.

Part B: NOT Seasonally Adjusted

Exhibit 17. Imports of Energy-Related Petroleum Products, Including Crude Oil

Details may not equal totals due to rounding.

Period	Total energy-related petroleum products (1)		Crude oil			
	Quantity (thousands of barrels)	Value (thousands of dollars)	Quantity (thousands of barrels)	Thousands of barrels per day (average)	Value (thousands of dollars)	Unit price (dollars)
2013						
Jan.- Dec.	3,549,956	352,082,357	2,813,770	7,709	272,807,177	96.95
Jan.- Nov.	3,264,860	325,386,802	2,583,459	7,735	251,772,797	97.46
January	327,865	31,766,772	261,631	8,440	24,597,165	94.01
February	263,093	26,033,893	206,101	7,361	19,741,207	95.78
March	280,583	28,149,793	216,817	6,994	20,986,387	96.79
April	297,503	29,785,453	234,663	7,822	22,934,878	97.74
May	312,431	30,909,911	241,406	7,787	23,353,282	96.74
June	291,633	28,752,500	234,749	7,825	22,739,548	96.87
July	325,999	32,339,647	263,196	8,490	25,547,504	97.07
August	303,792	31,033,309	240,153	7,747	24,079,030	100.27
September	289,784	30,015,728	229,580	7,653	23,417,961	102.00
October	306,144	30,955,410	242,422	7,820	24,232,134	99.96
November	266,034	25,644,385	212,742	7,091	20,143,703	94.69
December	285,095	26,695,555	230,311	7,429	21,034,380	91.33
2014						
Jan.- Nov.	3,068,107	293,409,551	2,453,508	7,346	228,190,547	93.01
January	311,606	29,073,951	256,518	8,275	23,141,406	90.21
February	264,514	25,185,466	212,524	7,590	19,452,786	91.53
March	289,676	28,257,593	225,039	7,259	21,133,737	93.91
April	297,175	29,303,921	238,789	7,960	22,799,437	95.48
May	279,613	27,956,136	213,143	6,876	20,487,021	96.12
June	267,192	26,599,392	213,931	7,131	20,625,563	96.41
July	293,953	29,323,258	238,736	7,701	23,351,167	97.81
August	271,322	26,622,325	215,367	6,947	20,744,812	96.32
September	275,988	26,010,134	226,487	7,550	20,960,194	92.54
October	279,141	25,089,810	224,101	7,229	19,826,783	88.47
November	237,927	19,987,564	188,873	6,296	15,667,641	82.95
December						

(1) Details shown for these Energy-Related Petroleum Products are not available on a BOP basis. These products include the following SITC commodity groupings: crude oil, petroleum preparations, and liquefied propane and butane gas.

NOTE: For information on data sources, nonsampling errors and definitions, see the information section on page A-1 of this release or at www.census.gov/ft900 or www.bea.gov/newsreleases/international/trade/tradnewsrelease.htm.

Part B: NOT Seasonally Adjusted

Exhibit 18. Exports and Imports of Motor Vehicles and Parts by Selected Countries: 2014

In millions of dollars. Details may not equal totals due to rounding. (X) Not applicable. (-) Represents zero or less than one-half of the measurement shown.

Country	Total			Passenger Cars			Trucks, Buses, Special Purpose Vehicles			Parts		
	November	October	Year-to-Date	November	October	Year-to-Date	November	October	Year-to-Date	November	October	Year-to-Date
Exports												
TOTAL	13,593	14,908	150,264	4,743	5,261	55,423	1,825	1,963	19,993	7,025	7,684	74,848
Australia	303	360	3,484	177	197	1,865	31	60	455	95	103	1,164
Belgium	84	78	840	44	31	313	4	3	38	36	44	489
Brazil	100	127	1,351	37	31	290	3	6	157	60	91	903
Canada	5,103	5,397	55,693	1,094	1,185	13,318	1,297	1,324	14,250	2,712	2,888	28,125
Chile	110	77	1,117	19	28	367	60	22	421	31	28	329
China	1,049	1,260	12,772	806	994	10,262	17	14	130	226	252	2,380
Colombia	47	78	639	17	18	260	2	32	80	27	27	300
France	56	58	640	15	19	197	1	(-)	18	40	39	425
Germany	602	712	7,057	446	520	5,196	6	7	78	150	185	1,783
Hong Kong	96	83	1,055	31	26	312	1	(-)	3	64	57	740
Japan	181	200	2,000	65	64	635	6	6	57	111	129	1,308
Korea, South	206	195	1,793	106	116	905	17	4	39	84	76	848
Kuwait	72	67	709	65	53	586	3	9	67	5	5	57
Mexico	3,005	3,351	32,140	322	335	3,430	129	154	1,279	2,553	2,862	27,430
Nigeria	95	95	989	74	76	800	14	12	109	8	7	80
Russia	144	210	2,008	84	146	1,429	10	6	76	50	58	503
Saudi Arabia	290	325	4,028	236	271	3,382	25	27	309	29	28	336
Singapore	29	36	352	1	1	8	1	1	15	27	35	328
South Africa	56	81	981	22	11	239	11	42	474	23	28	267
United Arab Emirates	336	327	3,241	245	225	2,425	15	26	197	76	75	618
United Kingdom	279	342	3,013	159	205	1,667	5	4	46	115	134	1,300
Venezuela	62	78	463	21	14	64	14	8	66	27	57	333
Other	1,289	1,372	13,900	656	697	7,472	155	198	1,626	477	478	4,801
Imports												
TOTAL	28,260	30,559	302,029	13,935	13,939	139,690	2,879	3,216	29,608	11,446	13,404	132,731
Austria	155	170	2,018	58	50	694	(-)	(-)	3	97	119	1,321
Brazil	80	103	1,072	(-)	1	5	6	7	77	74	95	991
Canada	5,522	5,946	57,621	3,932	4,059	39,112	240	266	2,179	1,350	1,621	16,330
China	1,463	1,655	17,165	13	14	118	28	30	235	1,421	1,612	16,812
Germany	3,402	3,367	33,810	2,513	2,352	23,678	30	33	279	859	982	9,853
Italy	392	439	3,458	263	281	2,002	(-)	1	8	128	158	1,448
Japan	4,213	4,479	46,051	2,965	2,940	30,830	61	59	555	1,188	1,480	14,666
Korea, South	2,021	1,928	21,061	1,270	1,101	13,067	(-)	(-)	2	751	827	7,991
Mexico	8,184	9,445	89,677	1,786	2,042	19,423	2,373	2,642	24,596	4,024	4,762	45,658
South Africa	161	168	1,571	119	128	1,142	(-)	(-)	(-)	41	40	429
Sweden	81	148	1,417	43	84	739	7	17	274	32	47	404
Taiwan	243	271	2,849	8	14	69	1	2	18	234	255	2,762
Thailand	193	219	2,031	17	17	160	1	(-)	2	175	201	1,870
United Kingdom	655	613	6,457	512	421	4,628	39	72	540	104	120	1,288
Other	1,496	1,607	15,772	435	437	4,023	93	86	841	968	1,084	10,909

NOTE: Data are not available on a BOP basis. For information on data sources, nonsampling errors and definitions, see the information section on page A-1 of this release or at www.census.gov/ft900 or www.bea.gov/newsreleases/international/trade/tradnewsrelease.htm.

Part C: Seasonally Adjusted (by Geography)

Exhibit 19. U.S. Trade in Goods by Selected Countries and Areas - Census Basis

In millions of dollars. (R) - Revised.

Country and Area	November 2014	October 2014	Third Quarter 2013	Fourth Quarter 2013	First Quarter 2014	Second Quarter 2014	Third Quarter 2014	Year-to-Date 2014	Year-to-Date 2013
Balance									
Brazil	619	792	4,088	3,884	4,613	3,491	2,291	11,806	14,906
Canada	-1,375	(R) -2,669	-8,656	-7,112	-7,103	-9,524	-9,933	-30,604	-28,757
China	-29,762	-29,572	-81,148	-79,507	-79,929	-85,272	-87,280	-311,814	-291,282
France	-1,561	-990	-3,319	-3,484	-4,614	-4,067	-3,519	-14,752	-12,667
Germany	-6,322	-6,263	-17,447	-17,137	-17,354	-19,175	-19,045	-68,159	-61,733
India	-1,695	-2,016	-5,082	-5,294	-5,984	-6,004	-5,842	-21,541	-17,976
Italy	-2,304	-2,158	-5,288	-5,945	-5,637	-6,467	-6,316	-22,882	-19,985
Japan	-5,583	-5,862	-18,552	-17,132	-16,907	-17,217	-16,040	-61,609	-67,747
Korea, South	-2,892	-2,419	-5,368	-3,919	-5,235	-6,046	-5,903	-22,494	-19,279
Mexico	-4,428	-5,411	-14,084	-13,411	-12,286	-12,344	-13,785	-48,255	-49,846
Saudi Arabia	-1,328	-1,176	-9,109	-9,457	-11,581	-8,127	-5,419	-27,631	-29,669
United Kingdom	-230	309	-1,491	-1,491	-1,720	-246	1,699	-189	-4,655
All other countries	97	-3,853	-8,896	-8,087	-12,637	-11,420	-9,564	-37,376	-44,001
CAFTA-DR	474	464	169	91	415	251	1,052	2,655	-464
European Union	-12,744	-11,241	-30,195	-33,935	-32,290	-37,370	-34,508	-128,153	-114,353
Newly Industrialized Countries	411	1,951	3,768	6,036	4,610	1,764	1,934	10,671	14,731
OPEC	-1,552	-2,231	-18,117	-16,598	-20,602	-12,697	-10,380	-47,461	-62,877
South/Central America	4,276	2,298	7,903	7,399	7,022	8,632	9,675	31,904	22,602
Exports									
Brazil	3,261	3,572	11,556	10,588	11,545	10,732	10,218	39,329	40,331
Canada	26,719	(R) 26,740	75,295	77,419	74,227	78,126	80,712	286,523	276,036
China	11,115	11,363	29,017	35,308	31,707	29,143	29,448	112,776	110,065
France	2,360	2,734	8,403	8,503	7,422	8,122	7,974	28,612	28,866
Germany	3,874	3,782	11,822	11,889	12,963	12,445	12,496	45,561	43,542
India	2,343	1,913	5,278	5,091	5,180	4,930	5,353	19,720	20,240
Italy	1,425	1,456	4,443	4,188	4,361	4,011	4,304	15,557	15,325
Japan	5,029	5,408	16,318	16,405	17,220	16,412	17,126	61,196	59,836
Korea, South	3,705	3,596	10,086	11,468	11,217	11,207	11,140	40,864	37,914
Mexico	20,215	20,023	56,611	57,544	58,642	60,967	60,865	220,712	206,793
Saudi Arabia	1,472	1,530	4,443	4,707	4,158	4,788	4,762	16,709	17,295
United Kingdom	4,306	4,619	11,665	11,649	11,692	13,736	14,813	49,167	43,842
All other countries	51,299	49,844	148,881	147,860	149,527	151,724	151,437	553,831	546,355
CAFTA-DR	2,630	2,667	7,689	7,601	7,816	7,909	7,889	28,913	27,113
European Union	22,219	22,941	67,405	65,962	67,716	70,873	70,851	254,600	241,017
Newly Industrialized Countries	11,781	13,000	34,734	36,095	36,641	35,227	34,871	131,520	128,430
OPEC	6,889	7,236	19,994	19,870	18,797	20,856	21,835	75,614	77,943
South/Central America	15,504	15,003	47,671	45,649	45,850	46,258	47,479	170,095	168,406
Imports									
Brazil	2,642	2,780	7,468	6,704	6,931	7,242	7,927	27,523	25,425
Canada	28,094	29,409	83,951	84,531	81,331	87,649	90,644	317,127	304,793
China	40,877	40,935	110,165	114,815	111,636	114,415	116,728	424,590	401,347
France	3,921	3,724	11,723	11,987	12,036	12,189	11,493	43,364	41,534
Germany	10,196	10,045	29,269	29,026	30,317	31,621	31,541	113,720	105,275
India	4,038	3,930	10,360	10,385	11,164	10,935	11,195	41,262	38,216
Italy	3,729	3,615	9,731	10,133	9,998	10,477	10,620	38,439	35,310
Japan	10,613	11,270	34,870	33,537	34,127	33,629	33,166	122,805	127,583
Korea, South	6,597	6,014	15,454	15,387	16,452	17,252	17,043	63,359	57,193
Mexico	24,644	25,434	70,695	70,955	70,928	73,312	74,650	268,967	256,638
Saudi Arabia	2,800	2,705	13,552	14,163	15,739	12,915	10,180	44,340	46,964
United Kingdom	4,536	4,310	13,157	13,140	13,412	13,983	13,114	49,355	48,497
All other countries	51,202	53,697	157,778	155,947	162,163	163,144	161,001	591,207	590,356
CAFTA-DR	2,157	2,203	7,520	7,510	7,402	7,659	6,838	26,258	27,577
European Union	34,963	34,182	97,600	99,897	100,006	108,243	105,358	382,753	355,370
Newly Industrialized Countries	11,370	11,049	30,966	30,059	32,032	33,462	32,937	120,849	113,699
OPEC	8,441	9,468	38,110	36,468	39,399	33,553	32,215	123,075	140,821
South/Central America	11,228	12,705	39,768	38,249	38,828	37,626	37,804	138,191	145,804

NOTES:
* Countries may be included in more than one area. For a list of countries in each area, see the information section on page A-1 of this release or at www.census.gov/ft900 or www.bea.gov/newsreleases/international/trade/tradnewsrelease.htm.
* Area data reflect the composition of the areas as they were as of the most recent statistical period.
* Seasonally adjusted country and area data in this exhibit will not sum to the commodity-based seasonally adjusted totals shown in Part A of this release. Data users should use caution drawing comparisons between the two sets of seasonally adjusted series.
* For information on data sources, nonsampling errors and definitions, see the information section on page A-1 of this release or at www.census.gov/ft900 or www.bea.gov/newsreleases/international/trade/tradnewsrelease.htm.

Part C: Seasonally Adjusted (by Geography)

Exhibit 20. U.S. Trade in Goods and Services by Selected Countries and Areas - BOP Basis

In millions of dollars.

Country and Area	Second Quarter 2013	Third Quarter 2013	Fourth Quarter 2013	First Quarter 2014	Second Quarter 2014	Third Quarter 2014	Annual 2011	Annual 2012	Annual 2013
Balance									
Brazil	8,827	9,079	8,762	9,795	8,327	7,735	27,667	29,252	36,145
Canada	-485	-1,676	19	-424	-2,582	-2,918	-10,683	-5,071	-2,508
China	-72,105	-74,498	-73,583	-73,483	-78,083	-80,420	-278,533	-295,293	-295,344
France	-2,493	-2,534	-2,478	-3,174	-2,922	-2,499	-11,198	-9,770	-10,255
Germany	-18,459	-19,220	-18,173	-18,688	-20,892	-20,555	-53,197	-65,441	-72,944
India	-6,391	-6,524	-6,507	-7,185	-7,361	-7,291	-20,278	-24,542	-25,360
Italy	-5,844	-5,532	-6,478	-6,144	-6,873	-6,743	-19,388	-23,247	-23,669
Japan	-15,016	-14,841	-13,492	-13,112	-14,037	-12,454	-45,426	-58,369	-58,491
Korea, South	-3,061	-1,947	-1,015	-2,300	-2,681	-3,285	-5,439	-7,689	-9,323
Mexico	-11,570	-12,488	-11,979	-11,406	-11,797	-13,190	-56,968	-53,993	-47,848
Saudi Arabia	-5,665	-6,999	-7,678	-9,494	-6,658	-3,797	-28,220	-30,911	-25,243
United Kingdom	2,015	1,658	1,364	1,107	2,986	4,968	14,806	11,357	7,041
All other countries	11,948	16,321	15,145	10,682	15,861	17,702	-61,767	-3,886	51,406
CAFTA-DR	n.a.	n.a.	n.a.	n.a.	n.a.	n.a.	n.a.	n.a.	n.a.
European Union	-20,073	-19,986	-23,877	-23,047	-24,995	-21,867	-58,543	-76,259	-84,542
Newly Industrialized Countries	8,667	10,916	12,085	11,060	9,674	8,475	34,688	33,387	40,969
OPEC	-12,409	-12,736	-12,269	-15,145	-7,725	-5,057	-113,430	-82,756	-49,419
South/Central America	11,768	14,858	14,473	13,380	15,749	17,281	11,996	30,994	53,928
Exports									
Brazil	17,440	18,194	17,265	18,375	17,696	17,365	66,165	68,623	70,712
Canada	90,518	91,349	93,559	90,224	94,109	96,960	340,997	355,623	366,329
China	38,226	39,494	44,976	42,077	40,433	40,299	133,880	144,879	160,599
France	12,855	13,200	13,471	12,748	13,507	13,046	47,141	49,115	51,577
Germany	18,626	18,568	19,246	20,131	19,502	19,619	76,829	76,270	75,251
India	9,262	8,709	8,786	8,751	8,641	8,995	33,436	34,626	35,695
Italy	6,389	7,023	6,505	6,868	6,504	6,824	25,475	24,947	26,248
Japan	28,381	28,163	28,337	29,202	28,339	29,089	111,080	118,009	112,782
Korea, South	15,304	16,363	17,171	16,845	17,129	16,524	61,883	62,322	64,408
Mexico	63,738	64,316	65,295	66,111	68,491	68,520	225,058	244,631	256,615
Saudi Arabia	7,232	6,995	6,853	6,598	6,626	6,774	20,561	25,935	28,011
United Kingdom	27,347	27,071	27,036	27,193	29,584	30,780	114,663	115,186	108,669
All other countries	230,525	231,327	230,196	232,288	238,309	237,280	869,852	896,374	923,299
CAFTA-DR	n.a.	n.a.	n.a.	n.a.	n.a.	n.a.	n.a.	n.a.	n.a.
European Union	117,627	119,319	118,367	121,355	126,472	126,523	472,935	468,846	471,566
Newly Industrialized Countries	47,985	49,791	50,188	50,981	51,052	49,445	186,950	188,781	196,801
OPEC	28,471	27,765	27,368	26,825	28,657	29,442	92,489	109,328	114,169
South/Central America	69,755	73,395	71,608	70,903	72,537	73,851	261,797	278,210	286,702
Imports									
Brazil	8,614	9,115	8,502	8,579	9,369	9,630	38,498	39,370	34,567
Canada	91,003	93,025	93,540	90,648	96,691	99,878	351,680	360,694	368,836
China	110,332	113,992	118,559	115,560	118,517	120,719	412,413	440,172	455,943
France	15,348	15,734	15,948	15,923	16,430	15,545	58,340	58,885	61,832
Germany	37,085	37,788	37,419	38,819	40,394	40,174	130,025	141,711	148,195
India	15,653	15,234	15,293	15,937	16,002	16,286	53,714	59,168	61,054
Italy	12,234	12,555	12,983	13,012	13,377	13,567	44,863	48,194	49,917
Japan	43,397	43,004	41,829	42,314	42,376	41,544	156,506	176,378	171,273
Korea, South	18,364	18,310	18,186	19,146	19,810	19,809	67,322	70,012	73,731
Mexico	75,307	76,804	77,273	77,517	80,288	81,710	282,027	298,625	304,463
Saudi Arabia	12,896	13,994	14,531	16,092	13,283	10,571	48,781	56,846	53,254
United Kingdom	25,332	25,413	25,672	26,085	26,598	25,812	99,858	103,829	101,627
All other countries	218,577	215,006	215,051	221,606	222,448	219,577	931,619	900,261	871,893
CAFTA-DR	n.a.	n.a.	n.a.	n.a.	n.a.	n.a.	n.a.	n.a.	n.a.
European Union	137,700	139,305	142,244	144,402	151,467	148,390	531,477	545,105	556,108
Newly Industrialized Countries	39,319	38,876	38,103	39,921	41,378	40,970	152,262	155,394	155,832
OPEC	40,880	40,502	39,637	41,970	36,382	34,499	205,919	192,084	163,588
South/Central America	57,986	58,536	57,135	57,523	56,788	56,570	249,802	247,216	232,775

n.a. Not available

NOTES:

* Countries may be included in more than one area. For a list of countries in each area and for additional information on country and area detail for goods on a BOP basis and for services, see the information section on page A-1 of this release or at www.census.gov/ft900 or www.bea.gov/newsreleases/international/trade/tradnewsrelease.htm.

* Area data reflect the composition of the areas as they were at the time of reporting.

* Seasonally adjusted country and area data in this exhibit will not sum to the seasonally adjusted totals shown in Part A of this release. Data users should use caution drawing comparisons between the two sets of seasonally adjusted series.

* For information on data sources, nonsampling errors and definitions, see the information section that begins on page A-1 of this release or at www.census.gov/ft900 or www.bea.gov/newsreleases/international/trade/tradnewsrelease.htm.

Part C: Seasonally Adjusted (by Geography)

Exhibit 20a. U.S. Trade in Goods by Selected Countries and Areas - BOP Basis

In millions of dollars.

Country and Area	Second Quarter 2013	Third Quarter 2013	Fourth Quarter 2013	First Quarter 2014	Second Quarter 2014	Third Quarter 2014	Annual 2011	Annual 2012	Annual 2013
Balance									
Brazil	3,954	4,235	3,954	4,681	3,608	2,656	11,357	11,757	16,852
Canada	-8,725	-9,697	-8,360	-8,483	-10,791	-11,225	-38,484	-35,804	-35,336
China	-77,614	-80,761	-80,022	-80,128	-85,178	-86,940	-295,187	-315,010	-318,778
France	-3,741	-3,506	-3,633	-4,570	-4,119	-3,559	-12,348	-11,138	-14,524
Germany	-17,082	-17,612	-17,273	-17,584	-19,404	-19,163	-50,239	-61,076	-67,600
India	-5,083	-5,092	-5,100	-5,927	-5,971	-5,834	-14,682	-18,397	-19,789
Italy	-5,397	-5,337	-6,040	-5,688	-6,509	-6,348	-18,093	-21,093	-22,196
Japan	-19,016	-18,929	-17,385	-17,321	-17,795	-16,335	-64,555	-77,690	-74,755
Korea, South	-5,441	-5,077	-3,589	-4,919	-5,612	-5,564	-12,368	-15,250	-19,471
Mexico	-14,698	-15,544	-14,754	-14,054	-14,010	-15,569	-68,741	-66,729	-59,937
Saudi Arabia	-7,647	-9,171	-9,564	-11,711	-8,167	-5,812	-33,469	-37,767	-33,121
United Kingdom	-1,311	-1,477	-1,487	-1,922	-220	1,594	4,489	-319	-5,448
All other countries	-12,393	-8,998	-8,626	-13,482	-10,969	-9,615	-148,325	-93,578	-47,565
CAFTA-DR	-650	55	2	354	180	944	1,338	-1,367	-817
European Union	-30,717	-30,162	-34,027	-33,707	-37,625	-34,247	-101,634	-118,006	-126,916
Newly Industrialized Countries	3,320	4,510	6,636	5,300	2,483	2,448	17,296	14,225	18,493
OPEC	-17,452	-18,321	-17,878	-21,157	-12,814	-10,821	-129,098	-101,598	-70,827
South/Central America	4,671	7,881	7,226	6,915	8,641	9,820	-5,626	10,865	25,677
Exports									
Brazil	10,761	11,560	10,574	11,539	10,725	10,228	42,895	43,577	44,072
Canada	74,685	75,700	77,617	74,536	78,449	81,087	282,678	294,090	303,048
China	29,135	29,679	35,057	31,872	29,648	30,201	105,445	111,789	122,838
France	7,725	8,447	8,594	7,522	8,220	8,087	28,420	31,257	32,089
Germany	11,693	11,900	11,975	13,026	12,522	12,596	49,758	49,266	47,722
India	5,848	5,319	5,327	5,264	5,020	5,416	21,656	22,276	22,225
Italy	4,151	4,485	4,211	4,415	4,054	4,340	16,276	16,231	16,896
Japan	16,823	16,636	16,781	17,450	16,691	17,432	67,251	71,480	66,512
Korea, South	10,261	10,562	11,897	11,617	11,702	11,592	45,219	44,337	43,504
Mexico	56,268	56,727	57,849	58,705	61,085	61,002	198,622	216,426	226,760
Saudi Arabia	4,964	4,399	4,624	4,043	4,769	4,397	14,096	17,989	18,770
United Kingdom	12,238	11,932	11,922	11,901	13,937	14,990	57,350	56,012	48,400
All other countries	150,065	150,400	149,038	150,539	153,508	152,487	569,573	586,959	599,947
CAFTA-DR	6,997	7,665	7,599	7,833	7,917	7,873	30,353	29,884	29,654
European Union	65,926	68,219	66,782	68,544	71,690	71,701	273,712	269,397	265,654
Newly Industrialized Countries	34,992	35,797	36,893	37,560	36,253	35,667	141,396	139,296	143,588
OPEC	21,009	19,727	19,352	18,500	21,087	21,222	65,225	80,765	83,093
South/Central America	44,625	47,856	45,747	46,016	46,443	47,606	169,925	183,704	185,094
Imports									
Brazil	6,807	7,325	6,620	6,858	7,117	7,572	31,539	31,820	27,221
Canada	83,410	85,397	85,977	83,019	89,240	92,311	321,163	329,894	338,384
China	106,749	110,440	115,079	112,000	114,826	117,141	400,632	426,799	441,616
France	11,465	11,953	12,226	12,092	12,339	11,646	40,769	42,395	46,613
Germany	28,775	29,511	29,248	30,610	31,926	31,759	99,997	110,342	115,323
India	10,931	10,411	10,428	11,191	10,991	11,249	36,338	40,673	42,014
Italy	9,548	9,822	10,251	10,103	10,563	10,688	34,369	37,324	39,092
Japan	35,839	35,565	34,165	34,771	34,486	33,767	131,806	149,170	141,267
Korea, South	15,702	15,639	15,486	16,536	17,313	17,155	57,587	59,587	62,975
Mexico	70,967	72,271	72,603	72,759	75,095	76,571	267,364	283,155	286,697
Saudi Arabia	12,612	13,570	14,187	15,754	12,936	10,208	47,565	55,756	51,891
United Kingdom	13,549	13,409	13,410	13,823	14,156	13,396	52,861	56,332	53,849
All other countries	162,458	159,398	157,664	164,021	164,477	162,102	717,897	680,537	647,512
CAFTA-DR	7,647	7,611	7,597	7,479	7,737	6,929	29,014	31,251	30,471
European Union	96,642	98,382	100,809	102,251	109,315	105,948	375,346	387,403	392,570
Newly Industrialized Countries	31,673	31,288	30,258	32,260	33,771	33,220	124,100	125,072	125,095
OPEC	38,461	38,049	37,229	39,657	33,902	32,043	194,323	182,364	153,920
South/Central America	39,953	39,975	38,521	39,101	37,803	37,785	175,552	172,839	159,417

NOTES:

* Countries may be included in more than one area. For a list of countries in each area and for additional information on country and area detail for goods on a BOP basis and for services, see the information section on page A-1 of this release or at www.census.gov/ft900 or www.bea.gov/newsreleases/international/trade/tradnewsrelease.htm.

* Area data reflect the composition of the areas as they were at the time of reporting.

* Seasonally adjusted country and area data in this exhibit will not sum to the seasonally adjusted totals shown in Part A of this release. Data users should use caution drawing comparisons between the two sets of seasonally adjusted series.

* For information on data sources, nonsampling errors and definitions, see the information section that begins on page A-1 of this release or at www.census.gov/ft900 or www.bea.gov/newsreleases/international/trade/tradnewsrelease.htm.

Part C: Seasonally Adjusted (by Geography)

Exhibit 20b. U.S. Trade in Services by Selected Countries and Areas

In millions of dollars.

Country and Area	Second Quarter 2013	Third Quarter 2013	Fourth Quarter 2013	First Quarter 2014	Second Quarter 2014	Third Quarter 2014	Annual 2011	Annual 2012	Annual 2013
Balance									
Brazil	4,873	4,844	4,809	5,114	4,718	5,079	16,310	17,496	19,293
Canada	8,240	8,021	8,379	8,059	8,209	8,307	27,801	30,733	32,829
China	5,509	6,263	6,439	6,644	7,095	6,520	16,654	19,717	23,434
France	1,248	972	1,155	1,396	1,197	1,060	1,150	1,368	4,269
Germany	-1,376	-1,608	-900	-1,104	-1,488	-1,392	-2,958	-4,366	-5,344
India	-1,308	-1,433	-1,407	-1,258	-1,390	-1,457	-5,596	-6,145	-5,571
Italy	-447	-195	-439	-456	-363	-395	-1,295	-2,155	-1,473
Japan	4,000	4,089	3,892	4,209	3,757	3,881	19,130	19,321	16,264
Korea, South	2,380	3,130	2,574	2,619	2,930	2,279	6,928	7,561	10,148
Mexico	3,129	3,056	2,776	2,648	2,213	2,379	11,773	12,736	12,089
Saudi Arabia	1,983	2,172	1,886	2,217	1,509	2,015	5,248	6,857	7,878
United Kingdom	3,325	3,136	2,851	3,029	3,206	3,374	10,317	11,676	12,490
All other countries	24,342	25,319	23,770	24,164	26,830	27,317	86,558	89,692	98,971
CAFTA-DR	n.a.	n.a.	n.a.	n.a.	n.a.	n.a.	n.a.	n.a.	n.a.
European Union	10,644	10,176	10,151	10,659	12,629	12,380	43,091	41,747	42,374
Newly Industrialized Countries	5,347	6,406	5,449	5,760	7,192	6,028	17,392	19,163	22,476
OPEC	5,043	5,585	5,609	6,012	5,089	5,764	15,668	18,842	21,408
South/Central America	7,097	6,977	7,247	6,464	7,108	7,460	17,622	20,129	28,251
Exports									
Brazil	6,679	6,634	6,691	6,836	6,970	7,137	23,270	25,046	26,640
Canada	15,833	15,649	15,942	15,688	15,660	15,874	58,319	61,533	63,281
China	9,092	9,815	9,919	10,205	10,786	10,099	28,435	33,090	37,761
France	5,130	4,753	4,877	5,227	5,288	4,959	18,721	17,858	19,488
Germany	6,933	6,669	7,271	7,105	6,980	7,023	27,070	27,004	27,529
India	3,414	3,390	3,459	3,487	3,621	3,580	11,780	12,350	13,470
Italy	2,239	2,538	2,294	2,453	2,450	2,484	9,199	8,716	9,352
Japan	11,558	11,527	11,556	11,752	11,648	11,658	43,830	46,529	46,270
Korea, South	5,043	5,801	5,275	5,229	5,427	4,933	16,664	17,986	20,904
Mexico	7,469	7,589	7,446	7,406	7,406	7,519	26,436	28,205	29,855
Saudi Arabia	2,267	2,596	2,229	2,555	1,857	2,377	6,465	7,947	9,240
United Kingdom	15,109	15,140	15,114	15,292	15,647	15,790	57,314	59,173	60,269
All other countries	80,461	80,928	81,158	81,749	84,801	84,792	300,280	309,415	323,352
CAFTA-DR	n.a.	n.a.	n.a.	n.a.	n.a.	n.a.	n.a.	n.a.	n.a.
European Union	51,701	51,099	51,585	52,811	54,781	54,822	199,223	199,449	205,912
Newly Industrialized Countries	12,993	13,994	13,294	13,421	14,799	13,778	45,554	49,485	53,213
OPEC	7,461	8,038	8,016	8,325	7,570	8,220	27,263	28,562	31,076
South/Central America	25,130	25,538	25,861	24,887	26,094	26,245	91,872	94,506	101,608
Imports									
Brazil	1,807	1,790	1,882	1,722	2,252	2,058	6,959	7,550	7,347
Canada	7,593	7,628	7,563	7,629	7,451	7,567	30,518	30,799	30,452
China	3,583	3,551	3,480	3,560	3,691	3,579	11,781	13,373	14,327
France	3,883	3,781	3,722	3,831	4,091	3,899	17,571	16,490	15,219
Germany	8,309	8,277	8,172	8,209	8,468	8,415	30,028	31,369	32,873
India	4,722	4,823	4,865	4,745	5,011	5,037	17,376	18,495	19,041
Italy	2,686	2,733	2,732	2,909	2,813	2,879	10,494	10,871	10,825
Japan	7,557	7,439	7,664	7,543	7,891	7,777	24,700	27,208	30,006
Korea, South	2,662	2,671	2,701	2,610	2,497	2,654	9,735	10,424	10,756
Mexico	4,340	4,533	4,670	4,758	5,193	5,139	14,663	15,469	17,766
Saudi Arabia	285	423	343	338	347	363	1,217	1,090	1,362
United Kingdom	11,783	12,004	12,262	12,263	12,441	12,416	46,997	47,497	47,779
All other countries	56,119	55,609	57,388	57,585	57,971	57,476	213,722	219,723	224,381
CAFTA-DR	n.a.	n.a.	n.a.	n.a.	n.a.	n.a.	n.a.	n.a.	n.a.
European Union	41,057	40,923	41,434	42,151	42,152	42,442	156,132	157,702	163,538
Newly Industrialized Countries	7,646	7,588	7,845	7,661	7,607	7,750	28,162	30,322	30,737
OPEC	2,419	2,453	2,407	2,312	2,481	2,456	11,596	9,720	9,668
South/Central America	18,033	18,561	18,614	18,422	18,986	18,785	74,250	74,377	73,357

n.a. Not available

NOTES:

* Countries may be included in more than one area. For a list of countries in each area and for additional information on country and area detail for goods on a BOP basis and for services, see the information section on page A-1 of this release or at www.census.gov/ft900 or www.bea.gov/newsreleases/international/trade/tradnewsrelease.htm.

* Area data reflect the composition of the areas as they were at the time of reporting.

* Seasonally adjusted country and area data in this exhibit will not sum to the seasonally adjusted totals shown in Part A of this release. Data users should use caution drawing comparisons between the two sets of seasonally adjusted series.

* For information on data sources, nonsampling errors and definitions, see the information section that begins on page A-1 of this release or at www.census.gov/ft900 or www.bea.gov/newsreleases/international/trade/tradnewsrelease.htm.

INFORMATION ON GOODS AND SERVICES

GOODS (CENSUS BASIS)

Data for goods on a Census basis are compiled from the documents collected by the U.S. Customs and Border Protection and reflect the movement of goods between foreign countries and the 50 states, the District of Columbia, Puerto Rico, the U.S. Virgin Islands, and U.S. Foreign Trade Zones. They include government and non-government shipments of goods and exclude shipments between the United States and its territories and possessions; transactions with U.S. military, diplomatic, and consular installations abroad; U.S. goods returned to the United States by its Armed Forces; personal and household effects of travelers; and in-transit shipments. The General Imports value reflects the total arrival of merchandise from foreign countries that immediately enters consumption channels, warehouses, or Foreign Trade Zones.

For imports, the value reported is the U.S. Customs and Border Protection appraised value of merchandise—generally, the price paid for merchandise for export to the United States. Import duties, freight, insurance, and other charges incurred in bringing merchandise to the United States are excluded.

Exports are valued at the f.a.s. (free alongside ship) value of merchandise at the U.S. port of export, based on the transaction price including inland freight, insurance, and other charges incurred in placing the merchandise alongside the carrier at the U.S. port of exportation.

REVISION PROCEDURE (CENSUS BASIS)

Monthly Revisions: Monthly data include actual month's transactions as well as a small number of transactions for previous months. Each month, the U.S. Census Bureau revises the aggregate seasonally adjusted (current and real chained-dollar) and unadjusted export, import, and trade balance figures, as well as the end-use totals for the prior month. Country detail data and commodity detail data, based on the Standard International Trade Classification (SITC) Revision 4 and the North American Industry Classification System (NAICS), are not revised monthly. The timing adjustment shown in Exhibit 14 is the difference between monthly data as originally reported and as recompiled.

For October, exports of goods were revised upward less than $0.1 billion and imports of goods were revised downward $0.1 billion. Goods carry-over in November was $0.2 billion (0.1 percent) for exports and $1.4 billion (0.7 percent) for imports. For October, revised export carry-over was less than $0.1 billion and revised import carry-over was $0.1 billion (0.1 percent).

Quarterly Revisions to Chain-Weighted Dollar Series: For March, June, September, and December statistical month releases, revisions are made to the real chained-dollar series presented in Exhibits 10 and 11: the previous five months are revised to incorporate the Bureau of Labor Statistics' revisions to price indexes, which are used to produce the real chained-dollar series and to align Census data with data published by the U.S. Bureau of Economic Analysis (BEA) in the National Income and Product Accounts (NIPAs).

Annual Revisions: Each June, not seasonally adjusted goods data are revised to redistribute monthly data that arrived too late for inclusion in the month of transaction. In addition, revisions are made to reflect corrections received subsequent to the monthly revisions. Seasonally adjusted data are also revised to reflect recalculated seasonal and trading-day adjustments. These revisions are reflected in totals, end-use, commodity, and country summary data.

Other Revisions: For December and January statistical month releases, each prior month of the most recent full year is revised so that the totals of the seasonally adjusted months equal the annual totals.

U.S./CANADA DATA EXCHANGE AND SUBSTITUTION

Data for U.S. exports to Canada are derived from import data compiled by Canada. The use of Canada's import data to produce U.S. export data requires several alignments in order to compare the two series.

1. *Coverage* - Canadian imports are based on country of origin. U.S. goods shipped from a third country are included. U.S. exports exclude these foreign shipments. For November 2014, these shipments totaled $168.6 million. U.S. export coverage also excludes U.S. postal shipments to Canada. For November 2014, these shipments totaled $19.7 million.

   U.S. import coverage includes shipments of railcars and locomotives from Canada. Effective with January 2004 statistics, Canada excludes these shipments from its goods exports to the United States, therefore creating coverage differences between the two countries for these goods.

2. *Valuation* - Canadian imports are valued at the point of origin in the United States. However, U.S. exports are valued at the port of exit in the United States and include inland freight charges, making the U.S. export value slightly larger than the Canadian import value. Canada requires inland freight to be reported separately from the value of the goods. Combining the inland freight and the Canadian reported import value provides a consistent valuation for all U.S. exports. Inland freight charges for November 2014 accounted for 2.1 percent of the value of U.S. exports to Canada.

3. *Re-exports* - Unlike Canadian imports, which are based on country of origin, U.S. exports include re-exports of foreign goods. Therefore, the aggregate U.S. export figure is slightly larger than the Canadian import figure. For November 2014, re-exports to Canada were $4,239.9 million.

4. *Exchange Rate* - Average monthly exchange rates are applied to convert the published data to U.S. currency. For November 2014, the average exchange rate was 1.1325 Canadian dollars per U.S. dollar.

5. *Other* - There are other minor differences, such as rounding error, that are statistically insignificant.

Canadian Estimates: Effective with January 2001 statistics, the current month data for exports to Canada contain an estimate for late arrivals and corrections. The following month, this estimate is replaced, in the news release exhibits only, with the actual value of late receipts and corrections. This estimate improves the current month data for exports to Canada and treats late receipts for exports to Canada in a manner that is more consistent with the treatment of late receipts for exports to other countries.

NONSAMPLING ERRORS

The goods data are a complete enumeration of documents collected by the U.S. Customs and Border Protection and are not subject to sampling errors. Quality assurance procedures are performed at every stage of collection, processing, and tabulation. However, the data are still subject to several types of nonsampling errors. The most significant of these include reporting errors, undocumented shipments, timeliness, data capture errors, and errors in the estimation of low-valued transactions.

Reporting Errors: Reporting errors are mistakes or omissions made by importers, exporters, or their agents in their import or export declarations. Most errors involve missing or invalid commodity classification codes and missing or incorrect quantities or shipping weights. They have a negligible effect on aggregate import, export, and balance of trade statistics. However, they can affect the detailed commodity statistics.

Undocumented Shipments: Federal regulations require importers, exporters, or their agents to report all merchandise shipments above established exemption levels. The U.S. Census Bureau has determined that not all required documents are filed, particularly for exports.

Timeliness and Data Capture Errors: The U.S. Census Bureau captures import and export information from administrative documents and through various automated collection programs. Documents may be lost, and data may be incorrectly keyed, coded, or recorded. Transactions may be included in a subsequent month's statistics if received late.

Low-valued Transactions: The total values of transactions valued as much as or below $2,500 for exports and $2,000 ($250 for certain quota items) for imports are estimated for each country, using factors based on the ratios of low-valued shipments to individual country totals for past periods.

The U.S. Census Bureau recommends that data users incorporate this information into their analyses, as nonsampling errors could impact the conclusion drawn from the results. For a detailed discussion of errors affecting the goods data, see "U.S. Merchandise Trade Statistics: A Quality Profile," available at www.census.gov/foreign-trade/aip/quality_profile10032014.pdf or from the Economic Indicators Division, U.S. Census Bureau.

AREA GROUPINGS

North America: Canada, Mexico.

Dominican Republic-Central America-United States Free Trade Agreement (CAFTA-DR): Costa Rica, Dominican Republic, El Salvador, Guatemala, Honduras, Nicaragua.

Europe: Albania, Andorra, Armenia, Austria, Azerbaijan, Belarus, Belgium, Bosnia and Herzegovina, Bulgaria, Croatia, Cyprus, Czech Republic, Denmark, Estonia, Faroe Islands, Finland, France, Georgia, Germany, Gibraltar, Greece, Hungary, Iceland, Ireland, Italy, Kazakhstan, Kosovo, Kyrgyzstan, Latvia, Liechtenstein, Lithuania, Luxembourg, Macedonia, Malta, Moldova, Monaco, Montenegro, Netherlands, Norway, Poland, Portugal, Romania, Russia, San Marino, Serbia, Slovakia, Slovenia, Spain, Svalbard-Jan Mayen Island, Sweden, Switzerland, Tajikistan, Turkey, Turkmenistan, Ukraine, United Kingdom, Uzbekistan, Vatican City.

European Union: Austria, Belgium, Bulgaria, Croatia, Cyprus, Czech Republic, Denmark, Estonia, Finland, France, Germany, Greece, Hungary, Ireland, Italy, Latvia, Lithuania, Luxembourg, Malta, Netherlands, Poland, Portugal, Romania, Slovakia, Slovenia, Spain, Sweden, United Kingdom.

Euro Area: Austria, Belgium, Cyprus, Estonia, Finland, France, Germany, Greece, Ireland, Italy, Latvia, Luxembourg, Malta, Netherlands, Portugal, Slovakia, Slovenia, Spain.

Newly Industrialized Countries (NICs): Hong Kong, Korea (South), Singapore, Taiwan.

Pacific Rim: Australia, Brunei, China, Hong Kong, Indonesia, Japan, Korea (South), Macau, Malaysia, New Zealand, Papua New Guinea, Philippines, Singapore, Taiwan.

South/Central America: Anguilla, Antigua and Barbuda, Argentina, Aruba, Bahamas, Barbados, Belize, Bermuda, Bolivia, Brazil, British Virgin Islands, Cayman Islands, Chile, Colombia, Costa Rica, Cuba, Curacao, Dominica, Dominican Republic, Ecuador, El Salvador, Falkland Islands (Islas Malvinas), French Guiana, Grenada, Guadeloupe, Guatemala, Guyana, Haiti, Honduras, Jamaica, Martinique, Montserrat, Netherlands Antilles, Nicaragua, Panama, Paraguay, Peru, Sint Maarten, St. Kitts and Nevis, St. Lucia, St. Vincent and the Grenadines, Suriname, Trinidad and Tobago, Turks and Caicos Islands, Uruguay, Venezuela.

OPEC: Algeria, Angola, Ecuador, Iran, Iraq, Kuwait, Libya, Nigeria, Qatar, Saudi Arabia, United Arab Emirates, Venezuela.

Africa: Algeria, Angola, Benin, Botswana, British Indian Ocean Territories, Burkina Faso, Burundi, Cabo Verde, Cameroon, Central African Republic, Chad, Comoros, Congo (Brazzaville), Congo (Kinshasa), Djibouti, Egypt, Equatorial Guinea, Eritrea, Ethiopia, French Southern and Antarctic Lands, Gabon, Gambia, Ghana, Guinea, Guinea-Bissau, Ivory Coast, Kenya, Lesotho, Liberia, Libya, Madagascar, Malawi, Mali, Mauritania,

Mauritius, Mayotte, Morocco, Mozambique, Namibia, Niger, Nigeria, Reunion, Rwanda, St. Helena, Sao Tome and Principe, Senegal, Seychelles, Sierra Leone, Somalia, South Africa, South Sudan, Sudan, Swaziland, Tanzania, Togo, Tunisia, Uganda, Western Sahara, Zambia, Zimbabwe.

ADJUSTMENTS FOR SEASONAL AND TRADING-DAY VARIATIONS

Goods are initially classified under the Harmonized Commodity Description and Coding System (Harmonized System), which is an internationally accepted standard for the commodity classification of traded goods. The Harmonized System describes and measures the characteristics of the goods and is the basis for the systems used in the United States: Schedule B for exports and Harmonized Tariff Schedule for imports. Combining trade into approximately 140 export and 140 import end-use categories makes it possible to examine goods according to their principal uses (see Exhibits 7 and 8). These categories are used as the basis for computing the seasonal and trading-day adjusted data. These adjusted data are then summed to the six end-use aggregates for publication (see Exhibit 6). These data are provided to BEA, from the U.S. Census Bureau, for use in the NIPAs and in the U.S International Transactions Accounts (balance of payments accounts).

Exhibit 19 shows goods (Census Basis) that are seasonally adjusted for selected countries and world areas. Unlike the commodity-based adjustments discussed above, these adjustments are developed and applied directly at the country and world area levels. For total exports and imports, data users should refer to the commodity-based totals shown in the other exhibits. The seasonally adjusted country and world area data will not sum to the seasonally adjusted commodity-based totals because the seasonally adjusted country and world area data and the commodity-based totals are derived from different aggregations of the export and import data and from different seasonal adjustment models. Data users should use caution drawing comparisons between the two sets of seasonally adjusted series.

The seasonal adjustment procedure (X13-ARIMA-SEATS) is based on a model that estimates the monthly movements as percentages above or below the general level of series (unlike other methods that redistribute the actual series values over the calendar year). Because the data series for aircraft is highly variable, users studying data trends may wish to analyze aircraft separately from other trade.

ADJUSTMENTS FOR PRICE CHANGE

Data adjusted for seasonal variation on a real chained-dollar basis (2009 base year) are presented in Exhibits 10 and 11. This adjustment for price change is done using the Fisher chain-weighted methodology. The deflators are primarily based on the monthly price indexes published by the Bureau of Labor Statistics using techniques developed for the NIPAs by BEA.

PRINCIPAL COMMODITIES

Goods data appearing in Exhibit 15 are classified in terms of the SITC Revision 4, with the exception of agricultural and manufactured goods. Agricultural goods are defined by the U.S. Department of Agriculture (USDA); they consist of non-marine food products and other products of agriculture that have not passed through complex processes of manufacture. Manufactured goods conform to the NAICS; they consist of goods that have been mechanically, physically, or chemically transformed. USDA agricultural goods and NAICS manufactured goods are not mutually exclusive categories.

Re-exports are foreign merchandise entering the country as imports and then exported in substantially the same condition as when imported. Re-exports, included in overall export totals, appear as separate line items in Exhibit 15.

ADVANCED TECHNOLOGY PRODUCTS

About 500 of some 22,000 Schedule B and Harmonized Tariff Schedule classification codes used in reporting U.S. merchandise trade are identified as "advanced technology" codes, and they meet the following criteria:

1. The code contains products whose technology is from a recognized high technology field (e.g., biotechnology).

2. These products represent leading edge technology in that field.

3. Such products constitute a significant part of all items covered in the selected classification code.

The aggregation of the goods results in a measure of advanced technology trade that appears in Exhibits 16 and 16a. This product- and commodity-based measure of advanced technology differs from broader NAICS-based measures, which include all goods produced by a particular industry group, regardless of the level of technology embodied in the goods.

GOODS (BALANCE OF PAYMENTS BASIS) AND SERVICES

Quarterly and annual statistics for goods on a balance of payments (BOP) basis and for services are included in the U.S. International Transactions Accounts (ITAs), which are published by BEA in news releases in March, June, September, and December and in the *Survey of Current Business* in the January, April, July, and October issues. The next release of the ITAs is scheduled for March 19, 2015. The *Survey of Current Business* is available online at www.bea.gov/scb/index.htm.

GOODS (BALANCE OF PAYMENTS BASIS)

Goods on a Census basis are adjusted by BEA to a BOP basis to align the data with the concepts and definitions used to prepare the international and national economic accounts. These adjustments, which are applied separately to exports and imports, are necessary to supplement coverage of the Census data, to eliminate duplication of transactions recorded elsewhere in the international accounts, and to value transactions at market prices. They include both *additions* to and *deductions* from goods on a Census basis and are presented in this release as *net adjustments*. Adjustments that exhibit significant seasonal patterns are seasonally adjusted. BEA also publishes more detailed quarterly and annual statistics for *net adjustments* in ITA Table 2.4. U.S. International Trade in Goods, Balance of Payments Adjustments and in the January, April, July, and October issues of the *Survey of Current Business*.

The export adjustments include:

Exports under U.S. military sales contracts - This adjustment reflects the net amount of two separate adjustments. BEA first *deducts* goods identified in the Census data as exports under the U.S. Foreign Military Sales program. BEA then *adds* primary source data for these exports, which are reported to BEA by the U.S. Department of Defense.

Gold exports, nonmonetary - This *addition* is made for gold that is purchased by foreign official agencies from private dealers in the United States and held at the Federal Reserve Bank of New York. The Census data only include gold that leaves the U.S. customs territory.

Goods procured in U.S. ports by foreign carriers - This *addition* is made for foreign air and ocean carriers' fuel purchases in U.S. ports.

Net exports of goods under merchanting - This *addition* is made to include the net value of the purchase and subsequent resale of goods abroad without the goods entering the United States. Because these goods do not cross the U.S. customs frontier, their value is not recorded in the Census data.

Other adjustments to exports include:

Deductions for equipment repairs (parts and labor), developed motion picture film, and military grant-aid. *Additions* for sales of fish caught in U.S. territorial waters, exports of electricity to Mexico, private gift parcels, vessels and oil rigs for which ownership changes, valuation of software exports at market value, and low-value (below reporting threshold) transactions for 1999–2009 to phase in a revised Census Bureau low-value methodology that was implemented for goods on a Census basis beginning with statistics for 2010.

The import adjustments include:

Gold imports, nonmonetary - This *addition* is made for gold sold by foreign official agencies to private purchasers out of stock held at the Federal Reserve Bank of New York. The Census data only include gold that enters the U.S. customs territory.

Goods procured in foreign ports by U.S. carriers - This *addition* is made for U.S. air and ocean carriers' fuel purchases in foreign ports.

Imports by U.S. military agencies - This *addition* is made for purchases of goods abroad by U.S. military agencies, which are reported to BEA by the U.S. Department of

Defense. The Census data only include imports of goods by U.S. military agencies that enter the U.S. customs territory.

Inland freight in Canada and Mexico - This *addition* is made for inland freight in Canada and Mexico. Imports of goods from all countries should be valued at the customs value—the value at the foreign port of export including inland freight charges. For imports from Canada and Mexico, this should be the cost of the goods at the U.S. border. However, the customs value for imports for certain Canadian and Mexican goods is the point of origin in Canada or Mexico. BEA makes an *addition* for the inland freight charges of transporting these goods to the U.S. border to make the value comparable to the customs value reported for imports from other countries.

Other adjustments to imports include:

Deductions for equipment repairs (parts and labor), repairs to U.S. vessels abroad, and developed motion picture film. *Additions* for non-reported imports of locomotives and railcars, imports of electricity from Mexico, conversion of vessels for commercial use, valuation of software imports at market value, and low-value (below reporting threshold) transactions for 1999–2009 to phase in a revised Census Bureau low-value methodology that was implemented for goods on a Census basis beginning with statistics for 2010.

SERVICES

The services statistics cover transactions between foreign countries and the 50 states, the District of Columbia, Puerto Rico, the U.S. Virgin Islands, and other U.S. territories and possessions. Transactions with U.S. military, diplomatic, and consular installations abroad are excluded because these installations are considered to be part of the U.S. economy.

Services statistics are based on quarterly, annual, and benchmark surveys and information obtained from monthly government and industry reports. For categories for which monthly data are not available, monthly statistics are derived from quarterly statistics through temporal distribution, or interpolation. The interpolation methodology used by BEA is the modified Denton proportional first difference method. This method preserves the pattern of the monthly indicator series, if available, while satisfying the annual aggregation constraints. See "An Empirical Review of Methods for Temporal Distribution and Interpolation in the National Accounts" for more information. Services are seasonally adjusted when statistically significant seasonal patterns are present.

Services are shown in nine broad categories. The following is a brief description of the types of services included in each category:

Maintenance and repair services n.i.e. (not included elsewhere) - Consists of maintenance and repair services performed by residents of one country on goods that are owned by residents of another country. The repairs may be performed at the site of the repair facility or elsewhere. Excludes such services in which the cost is included in the price of the goods and is not billed separately or is declared as a part of the price of the goods on the import or export declaration filed with the U.S. Customs and Border Protection. Maintenance and repair of ships, aircraft, and other transport equipment are included under transport services, and maintenance and repair of computers are included under computer services.

Transport - Consists of transactions associated with moving people and freight from one location to another and includes related supporting and auxiliary services. Transport covers all modes of transportation, including air, sea, rail, road, space, and pipeline. Postal and courier services and port services, which cover cargo handling, storage and warehousing, and other related transport services, are also included.

Travel (for all purposes including education) - Includes goods and services acquired by nonresidents while abroad. A traveler is defined as a person who stays, or intends to stay, for less than one year in a country of which he or she is not a resident or as a nonresident whose purpose is to obtain education or medical treatment, no matter how long the stay. Purchases can be either for own use or for gifts to others. Travel is a transactor-based component that covers a variety of goods and services, primarily lodging, meals, transportation in the country of travel, amusement, entertainment, and gifts. Excludes air passenger services for travel between countries, which are included in *transport*, and goods for resale, which are included in goods.

Travel includes business and personal travel. Business travel covers goods and services acquired for use by persons whose primary purpose for travel is for business (including goods and services for which business travelers are reimbursed by employers). Business travel also includes expenditures by border, seasonal, and other short-term workers in their economy of employment. Personal travel covers travel for all non-business purposes, including for medical or educational purposes.

Insurance services - Includes the direct insurance services of providing life insurance and annuities, non-life (property and casualty) insurance, reinsurance, freight insurance, and auxiliary insurance services. Insurance is measured as gross premiums earned plus premium supplements less claims payable, with an adjustment for claims volatility. Premium supplements represent investment income from insurance reserves, which are attributed to policyholders who are treated as paying the income back to the insurer. Auxiliary insurance services include agents' commissions, brokerage services, insurance consulting services, actuarial services, and other insurance services.

Financial services - Includes financial intermediary and auxiliary services, except insurance services. These services include those normally provided by banks and other financial institutions. Services primarily include those for which an explicit commission or a fee is charged; implicit fees for bond transactions, measured as the difference between bid and ask prices, are also included. Services include securities brokerage and underwriting, financial management, financial advisory, and custody services;

credit and other credit-related services; and securities lending, electronic funds transfer, and other services.

Charges for the use of intellectual property n.i.e. - Includes charges for the use of proprietary rights, such as patents, trademarks, and copyrights, and charges for licenses to use, reproduce, distribute, and sell or purchase intellectual property.

Telecommunications, computer, and information services - Telecommunications services include the broadcast or transmission of sound, images, data, or other information by electronic means. These services do not include the value of the information transmitted. Computer services consist of hardware- and software-related services and data processing services. Sales of customized software and related use licenses, as well as licenses to use non-customized software with a periodic license fee, are also included, as is software downloaded or otherwise electronically delivered. Cross-border transactions in non-customized packaged software with a license for perpetual use are included in goods. Information services include news agency services, database services, and web search portals.

Other business services - Consists of research and development services, professional and management consulting services, and technical, trade-related, and other business services. Research and development services include services associated with basic and applied research and experimental development of new products and processes. Professional and management consulting services include legal services, accounting, management consulting, managerial services, public relations services, advertising, and market research. Amounts received by a parent company from its affiliates for general overhead expenses related to these services are included. Technical, trade-related, and other business services include architectural and engineering, construction, audio-visual, waste treatment, operational leasing, trade-related, and other business services.

Government goods and services n.i.e. - Includes goods and services supplied by and to enclaves, such as embassies, military bases, and international organizations; goods and services acquired from the host economy by diplomats, consular staff, and military personnel located abroad and their dependents; and services supplied by and to governments that are not included in other services categories. Services supplied by and to governments are classified to specific services categories when source data permit.

GOODS (BOP BASIS) AND SERVICES BY COUNTRY AND AREA

Monthly country and area detail is not available for goods on a BOP basis or for services. However, quarterly statistics on goods on a BOP basis and on services that are seasonally adjusted by geography are shown in Exhibit 20. Unlike the seasonal adjustments by commodity and by service type that are applied to the global totals, these adjustments are developed and applied directly at the country and world area levels. For total exports and imports, data users should refer to the by-commodity and by-service type totals shown in the other exhibits. The seasonally adjusted country and world area data will not sum to the seasonally adjusted by-commodity and by-service type totals because the two sets of statistics are derived from different aggregations of the export and import data and from different seasonal adjustment models. Data users should use caution drawing comparisons between the two sets of seasonally adjusted series.

The definitions of the world areas shown in Exhibit 20 are consistent with the definitions for goods on a Census basis (see *AREA GROUPINGS* above) with a few exceptions. For services, CAFTA-DR is not available because trade with this area's member countries cannot be separately identified. For goods on a BOP basis and for services, European Union and OPEC reflect the composition of the areas as they were at the time of reporting.

REVISION PROCEDURE (GOODS ON A BOP BASIS AND SERVICES)

Monthly Revisions: Each month, a preliminary estimate for the current month and a revised estimate for the immediately preceding month are released. After the initial revision, no further revisions are made to a month until more complete source data become available in March, June, September, and December.

Quarterly Revisions: The releases in March, June, September, and December contain revised estimates for the previous six months to incorporate more comprehensive and updated source data.

Annual Revisions: Each June, historical data are revised to incorporate newly available and revised source data, changes in definitions and classifications, and changes in estimation methods. Seasonally adjusted data are also revised to reflect recalculated seasonal and trading-day adjustments.

Other Revisions: The release in February contains revisions to goods for January through November of the most recent year and the release in March contains revisions to both goods and services for all months of the most recent year. These revisions result from forcing the seasonally adjusted months to equal the annual totals.

DATA AVAILABILITY

The U.S. International Trade in Goods and Services news release (FT-900) and the FT-900 Supplement are available at the following:

www.census.gov/ft900

www.bea.gov/newsreleases/international/trade/tradnewsrelease.htm

MONTHLY RELEASE SCHEDULE		
Statistical Month	**Date**	**Day**
November	01-07-15	Wednesday
December	02-05-15	Thursday
January	03-06-15	Friday
February	04-02-15	Thursday
March	05-05-15	Tuesday
April	06-03-15	Wednesday
May	07-07-15	Tuesday
June	08-05-15	Wednesday
July	09-03-15	Thursday
August	10-06-15	Tuesday
September	11-04-15	Wednesday
October	12-04-15	Friday